Salvation Basics

For this Life and the Next

STEVE EVANS

forerunner
MINISTRIES

forerunner
PUBLISHING

Savannah, Georgia

Salvation Basics: How to Get Saved and Stay Saved
The River of Peace Series; Vol. 3
2013 by Steve Evans

Distributed by Forerunners4Him,
  A division of Forerunner Ministries, Inc.
  4625 Sussex Place, Savannah, GA 31405
  Email: info@forerunners4him.org
  Website: www.forerunners4him.org

Published by Forerunner Ministries, Inc.
ISBN-13: 978-0615844183
ISBN-10: 0615844189

Cover and interior design by Forerunner Publishing, Savannah, Georgia.

Printed in the United States of America by CreateSpace.

TABLE OF CONTENTS

Chapters

Bonus Section

Healing Streams
Forerunners4Him
Books from Forerunner

CHAPTER 1

ARE YOU A SEEKER?

The most important task imaginable lies right in front of you. We are disconnected from our God and we know it. What will *you* do about it? Our lives are racing towards death and we know it. What will it be like *for you* to face a God you have never known? In the moments after death you will know the truth, but by then it will be too late to make any adjustments. The time to act is *now*!

There is neither wisdom nor honor in setting this all-encompassing assignment aside: If God *can* be known, we *must* know Him. If He is there, He certainly expects nothing less from us. What honor or reward can there be for selfish, ungrateful creatures that show no interest in their Creator? If God *can* be found, we *must* find Him! Even if we are not at all concerned about the next life, we would be wise to re-unite with One who can make this life on earth a heaven and not a hell. What wisdom is there in rejecting any possible source of divine assistance?

In Christian terms all of this is impossible. We are so completely lost, it would take God to "find" us; so totally blind, it would take God to open our eyes; so entirely separated, it would take God to restore us. We cannot lead ourselves completely out of the darkness that enshrouds us, nor free ourselves fully from the sins that enslave us. Don't let that stop you! Like miners trapped within the depths of the earth, we can hold fast to hope and send our desperate messages to the surface.

We can "grope" our way towards the light.[1] We can
seek Him whom we cannot see. We can cry out to Him
whom we cannot hear. All is not lost, just because we
are lost. Take heart from this: Jesus promised that "All
who seek *shall* find."[2] We *can* embrace the quest!

In the beginning of my journey I didn't know Jesus
Christ from Adam's house cat. At first my spiritual
quest only succeeded in getting me further lost! Yet, my
heart was crying out for God, for the living God. He
heard that silent plea and took pity. That story is told in
Rescued from Hell: An Odyssey of Deception and Discovery.
Had He not come to my rescue, this book could never
have been written. As it is, I have had the pleasure of
being a part of His rescue in many lives since then. I
have never yet seen Him fail to save those who are
crying out to Him and calling upon His Name. May
you, too, find Him to be more than you could ever have
dreamed possible.[3]

---

[1] That God actually expects that we should be seeking Him is made clear
by Paul: Acts 17:26-28: *That they should seek God, in the hope that they might
feel their way toward him and find him.*

[2] This promise to seekers is from Jesus Himself: Matthew 7:7-8: *Ask, and it
will be given to you; seek, and you will find...* Here is a confirming word
given by God through one of His prophets: Jeremiah 29:13-14: *You will
seek me and find me. When you seek me with all your heart.*

[3] Our Creator would be a small god indeed, if He only lived up to our
expectations. In fact our Mighty God intends to far surpass our hopes
and dreams: 1 Corinthians 2:9 WEB: *But as it is written, "Things which an
eye didn't see, and an ear didn't hear, which didn't enter into the heart of man,
These God has prepared for those who love him."*

CHAPTER 2

WHAT ARE THE SALVATION BASICS?

I plan to walk you through all of the main issues, beginning with why you need to be saved and continuing all the way through to what your first steps as a newborn Christian will be. First, however, I have to introduce you to the "salvation basics." This profound truth appears in every chapter. It is a divine key that will unlock doors to your understanding and reveal God's working in your life as a comprehensive whole.

"What must I do to get saved" and "How can I get to heaven?" are the essential questions of salvation in terms of eternal life. The answer to both is wrapped up in the extremely "good news" of our salvation basics found in Paul's letter to the Ephesians: *We are saved by grace through faith.*

> **For by grace you have been saved through faith, and that not of yourselves; it is the gift of God, not of works, that no one would boast.** Ephesians 2:8-9 WEB

The Basics Rule All of Life

These basics get you started, but the basics also keep you going! Once you get a satisfactory answer to those two elementary questions, you will quickly discover a few more:

- Is there anything I need to do to stay saved?
- How can I always be sure that I am saved?

- Can I lose my salvation?
- How can I stop sinning?
- How do I live now that I am saved?

The answer to these and all other daily life questions is the same: *You are saved by grace through faith!* That dual purpose may surprise you, but don't let it throw you. God has no need to alter His methods, as if one way might work for getting us to heaven, but not for helping us live a heavenly life on earth. His way is perfect![1] It is perfectly designed to work for our benefit.

Everything and anything you try to do to "save" yourself (in this life or for the next), will only end in failure. Such misplaced effort will also burden you with unnecessary stress all along the way, because you put the responsibility of rescuing your life on you rather than on God. That is trying to live by making Self into your savior. The truth is Self cannot save you from sin and death; neither can Self save you from your own failings as a person or from the many predicaments of life. We need God's salvation to reach us in both of these dimensions:

1. The Next Life. Getting us to heaven means God has to save us *from our sins.*

2. This Life. Getting a heavenly life into us while we are still on earth means God has to save us *from ourselves.*

God's laws found in the Bible (a.k.a. God's *Rule Book* for us) will show you what you need to do and what you need to avoid, but the law cannot give you the power to live within its boundaries. It certainly cannot give you the freedom to soar on wings of the Spirit.[2] For that you will need God's grace which is also found in the Bible (a.k.a. God's *Love Letter* to us). By His wisdom God foresaw that we could *only* be saved by His grace through faith. You simply have to learn to trust God that His way of saving you—for heaven and in this life—really works.

Getting to Know God

Fortunately, you can get saved without knowing much about God, except that you *want* to know Him and *need* Him to save you. However, you need to know that you cannot live in the fullness of joy and peace promised to you unless you get to know your God very well—well enough to keep trusting and obeying Him no matter what's going on. Here is an absolutely certain progression: To truly know Jesus is to love Him; to love Him is to trust Him; to trust Him is to follow Him. Making "progress" in the walk, therefore, *always* comes as we get to know Jesus (and God) better.[3]

Knowing God well is a lifelong quest! At times it requires determined work, the work of growing one's faith. Happily, we actually want to do that part of the work, because God gives us a love for Jesus and Jesus awakens in us a love for the Father and the Holy Spirit.

With these basics in mind, let us move on to consider why we need to be saved.

Prayer

God, I don't know yet if You are really there or who You truly are, but if You are out there, then I ask You to come to me and help me find You. I need You to save me. I also desire to know You, the true and living God. Prepare me to receive Your salvation. Reveal Your truths to me and keep leading me in the way of grace and faith. I want to believe in You. Help me overcome my unbelief!

---

[1] Psalm 18:30 WEB: *As for God, his way is perfect.*

[2] Romans 8:2-3: *For the law of the Spirit of life has set you free in Christ Jesus from the law of sin and death.*

[3] Being "introduced" to Jesus is just the beginning. Even towards the end of a lifetime of service, Paul's supreme desire was to get to know the Lord better: Philippians 3:7-8; 12-13: *I count everything as loss because of the surpassing worth of knowing Christ Jesus my Lord...*

CHAPTER 3

WHY DO I NEED TO BE SAVED?

No doubt you have your own reasons for wanting to be saved, or you wouldn't be reading this book and exploring salvation. However, it may be instructive to compare how your thinking has been tracking with the most common reasons why we need salvation.

Reason #1: Conscience and Moral Failure

Every honest person knows deep down that they are not living up to their own moral standards, much less the ones that God requires. We all have the moral law within us in the form of conscience, God's homing beacon, leading us to seek the One who gave it to us. *Conscience is also a warning light,* alerting us to the ways in which we are failing to live as we should. Try as we might we cannot keep our lives within the moral boundaries at all times.[1] We know that this is wrong and that it is without excuse in general terms however much we may seek to find excuses for specific failings.

Let's call this our moral failure. We really do need someone to help us live as the truly good people which we *could* be and can't help but believe that we *should* be. What went wrong? Why can't we fix it? Why is there no one around who can fix us? Sure, you can put a patch on it by trying harder, or you can deny the problem and pretend that you're fine. Still, you know that something is not right.[2]

This is the first reason why we need to be saved: so that we can live on earth as we were meant to live. But this problem—the problem of our moral failure—only gets worse when we consider what it means to come to the end of our life without a solution for it. *How do you face death with the nagging awareness of your moral failures troubling your conscience?*

Reason #2: The Inevitability of Death

The path of life invariably leads towards death. This gloomy fact is universal. We tend to bury our heads on this one, but let's face the facts for a moment. You are going to die one day. This cannot be avoided. *What's next? Are you ready for that?*

There are four main possibilities that people have imagined which nicely bypass the problem created by our moral failure.

1) The Big Sleep. Death is the end of existence. Nothing continues except the memory of you and some of the things you set in motion. Best case scenario? You "live on" in other people's memories for a while, until they too enter the sleep of unconscious termination. But at least you don't have to worry about answering for your misdeeds. There may be no dream of eternal bliss, but neither would there be the nightmare of endless torment. If this fantasy were true...

2) The Lobotomy. Life is a cycle and you will be recycled, though all your memories will be removed.

You don't really die. You are "reincarnated" i
another body — so that's a plus.[3] Also there is no hell-
like future torment you need to fear for living the
present life with on-going moral failures. You won't
even remember this life in your next life! So
whatever future version of you is fated to suffer for
your failures in this life, well, that's not really *your*
problem, is it? Your problem is working through the
suffering of the present life coming to you from
failures of the previous one which some other
(forgotten) version of you loused up.

3) The Sucker's Bet. There is a heaven of endless
perfection for you to enjoy. Everyone is going to go
there! In fact all paths lead to God and heaven. So
don't worry, be happy. There is no hell to fear, no
sins you have to avoid. God loves everyone too
much to allow anyone to suffer for sin. This belief
sounds too good to be true and it is. It is a foolish
shot in the dark, since you have to bet against your
own conscience which tells you that right will be
rewarded and wrong won't be. Conscience never
lies. Don't play against the odds on this one — they're
way too long.

4) Mindless Bliss. You merge with the vast ocean of
God's consciousness. This may sound pretty good on
the surface. You don't get punished for any of your
moral failures, misdeeds or bad attitudes. But you
do have to give up being *a real person*. Instead of
being the unique symphony of ever shifting thought,
emotion and action (which you are in this life when
the internal orchestra is in tune), you become a

going on into the endless reaches of time.
individual—as an actual person—entirely
xist. You have been swallowed up by the
ind. Good for the Mind, too bad for you.

; OK," you may be thinking. "I could
handle that." (No you couldn't. There would be no
you left to deal with it one way or the other, but let's
don't pause to debate this.) "What I can't handle is
the thought of being punished, of having to answer
to some maybe not-so-friendly God for having
messed up my life." That possibility is exactly why
we need to be looking for a savior—*now!*

What if there really is a fifth possibility at the end of
this life? What if there really is a God we will have to
face?[4] What if the guilt we wish we didn't feel is a
warning from conscience that our moral failure is going
to have to be answered for one day?[5] What if there is a
God who really does care how we chose to live our
lives? What if there really is a place or time of
punishment and a place or time of reward hidden on
the other side of the veil of death? Shouldn't you be
prepared for that—*just in case*?

5) Heaven and Hell. Life on earth is very short
compared to whatever life after earth will be. Where
do you want to spend the endless years? *How* do
you want to spend them? Will you be gloriously
aflame with holy love or will you be wretchedly
burning in the infernal fires? You can gamble on one
of the first four possibilities being right and hope
you luck out, but what if you don't?

A robust majority of all the people ever born on the planet have displayed a belief in the afterlife and carried a hearty suspicion that it is a place of reward, one way or the other. Where did they get that? From religion? No, certainly not! If religion is of *human* origin (as it is alleged that all are), then the common themes of religion are *our* ideas, not aberrant notions foisted upon us. We need look no further than ourselves to discover the true origin of beliefs about the afterlife. The "majority view" got it the same place we get it—from the sense of a moral law within our hearts and the *fact* of an awesome creation surrounding us.[6]

The Enlightenment philosopher Immanuel Kant was hardly an ardent follower of the Christian faith, though he drew heavily on many of its principles. At the conclusion of his *Critique of Practical Reason* he famously wrote:[7]

Two things fill the mind with ever new and increasing admiration and awe, the more often and steadily we reflect upon them: the starry heavens above me and the moral law within me.

We get our ideas of the afterlife as a place of reward and punishment from the inward sense of a moral law requiring the operations of an overseeing justice. We experience no conflict in wanting it applied to others; conscience, however, insists that it applies to us as well. And it is conscience, no less than the starry heavens, which points us to something or to Someone far bigger than ourselves, to which or to Whom we are ultimately accountable.[8]

Facing God's judgment upon us and coming out on the side of reward, rather than punishment is a primary reason why we need to be saved. We are going to need to have some help standing up to close scrutiny![9] This brings us to the third reason we need to be saved.

Reason #3: We Are Separated from God

If there is a way to be saved (and there is) then it could hardly be considered complete if it only satisfied reasons #1 and #2 above. Unquestionably, we need to be saved/helped so that we can live more fully the life we are meant to live in this life and yes, we need to be saved/rescued so that we can live in the place of reward and blessing in the next life.

This still leaves out the ultimate reason why we need to be saved: *We are separated from the One who created us!* We are cut off from even knowing the greatest Being in the universe. The truly astonishing thing about this immense tragedy is how "normal" it seems to us to be severed from our Creator. We don't know His Name, we can't see His Face, we can't sense His Presence, we can't hear His Voice, we can't feel His Heart, we can't enjoy His Company. Unless God chooses to open those lost pathways of communication and communion for us, there is nothing we can do to reinstate them.

Try as we might, unaided by God, we cannot penetrate the vast "cloud of unknowing" that surrounds the great Mystery of who God is. We need to be re-connected with our God! If the Christian religion is truly God-given (as we believe that it is) then "the God that we don't know" just happens to be the most loving, most joyful, most exciting, most beautiful Person imaginable. Not to know Him is the worst possible form of ignorance and loss. God save us from not knowing You!

That, my friend, is exactly what He wants to do!

Prayer

God, I have to be honest with You. I don't know You, but deep down I really do believe that this world has a Creator and deep down I know that I am not living with a completely clear conscience. All three of these reasons for seeking You apply to me! I don't want to have to face You at the end of my life with my moral failures hanging over me. I don't want to take a chance on those other "possible endings"—my heart is telling me that the Christian view of heaven and hell is the right one. And I don't want to go on living separated from You, if there is a way that we can be reunited. Please, calm my fears and increase my desire to know You that I may seek You with my whole heart. Reveal Yourself to me in ways that I can sense and understand. Help me want what You want and make me willing to surrender everything to You.

---

[1] See all of Romans 7 for Paul's profound insights into the moral struggle everyone faces: Romans 7:22-23: *For I delight in the law of God, in my inner being, but I see in my members another law waging war against the law of my mind and making me captive to the law of sin that dwells in my members.*

[2] The Biblical term for that "something" which is not right about us is sin. The scriptures say that we are all riddled with it: Romans 3:22-23: *For all have sinned and fall short of the glory of God.*

[3] Back in my pre-Christian days I did have an experience of what seemed like memories of past lives in the context of a supernatural encounter. However, later—*when the demons that entered me then were cast out*—I

realized where the memories had come from. Demons never forget the lives they have indwelt and they have been around a very long time. This part of my story is told in *Rescued from Hell* available at Amazon.com.

[4] Hebrews 9:27 AMP: *And just as it is appointed for [all] men once to die, and after that the [certain] judgment.*

[5] The Bible "pulls no punches" where the penalty for our moral failings is concerned: Romans 6:23: *For the wages of sin is death.*

[6] We are fully expected to "read the signs" left for us in the world around us and these signs are sufficient to point us to God: Romans 1:19-21: *For what can be known about God is plain to them, because God has shown it to them. For his invisible attributes, namely, his eternal power and divine nature, have been clearly perceived, ever since the creation of the world, in the things that have been made...*

[7] Kant, Immanuel. *Critique of Practical Reason* (1788) 5:161.33–6; tr. Guyer 1992, 1. This statement was chosen by his friends for Kant's tombstone.

[8] Acts 17:26-27; previously cited, p. 6.

[9] Romans 14:10-12: *For we will all stand before the judgment seat of God... So then each of us will give an account of himself to God.*

CHAPTER 4

WHO "QUALIFIES" FOR SALVATION?

The great thing about being saved by God through Jesus Christ is the very low bar. You don't have to jump high or jump through a lot of hoops. You don't have to jump through hoops at all! It's not about you and what you have to do. It is about God and what He wants to give you.

Jesus said that He only came for "those who were sick"—not the healthy.[1] The "healthy" have no interest in salvation because they don't believe that they have anything wrong with them. Even Jesus could not save people who had no use for Him or what He offered them. So if you know you need salvation, then you are one of the "sick" whom Jesus wants to save!

Nothing about You Can Disqualify You

But it gets better than that. There are actually four conditions by which we could be described—none of which are desirable—that "qualify" a person for God's love and for His saving help. Paul lists them for us in his letter to the Romans:[2]

1. The weak—those who ought to be able to do better and wish they could do better, but can't.

2. The ungodly—those who live as if living for God doesn't matter; those who don't care about God, only themselves.

3. The sinful—those who know what is wrong, but do it anyway; those who know how they ought to live, but won't.

4. Enemies of God—those who live as if God were their enemy; those who live in direct, intentional opposition to what (they believe) God desires; those who have been living for God's enemy, the devil, rather than God.

Could you see yourself in one or more of those descriptions? Don't be afraid to admit it. This is what "qualifies" you to receive the mercy of being saved by our loving Father! The truth is none of us deserved to be saved. None of us can be good enough long enough to merit salvation. We have all fallen far short of God's uncompromising standards.[3]

It takes a lot of love to want to save people like us, but our Father has it: God *is* love.[4] It takes a lot of grace and patience to want to help people like us get saved, live saved and stay staved all the way to heaven, but our Father has it: He *is* the "God of all grace"![5] It takes a lot of sacrifice to pay the penalty for all of our wrong ways and wrong doing, so that people like us can be saved, but Jesus was willing and able to do it: He *is* our all-sufficient Savior![6]

Take heart dear Christian (or soon to be Christian), whatever your condition may be, you have a God who is intent on saving you. He is fully prepared to do everything necessary to save you to "the uttermost." Jesus is even praying for you when you can't find the right way to pray for yourself.

Consequently, he is able to save to the uttermost those who draw near to God through him, since he always lives to make intercession for them. Hebrews 7:25

Prayer

Father, thank You for making it so clear in Your Word that You want to save someone like me. I've been seeing how far I have fallen short, how little real strength I have to do the right thing, and how little desire I have at times to live the way that I know You would want me to live. I have been so afraid that I could never qualify for Your love or for getting to heaven. Now, I'm beginning to see that no one qualifies, that it's not about our goodness, but Yours! Thank You for loving me so perfectly and for making a way for me to be saved through the sacrifice of Jesus.

---

[1] Mark 2:17: *Those who are well have no need of a physician, but those who are sick. I came not to call the righteous, but sinners.*

[2] Romans 5:6-10: *For while we were still weak, at the right time Christ died for the ungodly... but God shows his love for us in that while we were still sinners, Christ died for us. Since, therefore, we have now been justified by his blood, much more shall we be saved by him from the wrath of God. For if while we were enemies we were reconciled to God by the death of his Son, much more, now that we are reconciled, shall we be saved by his life.*

[3] We compare ourselves to each other; God compares us to what He created us to be before we fell into sin: Romans 3:10-12: *None is righteous, no, not one; no one understands; no one seeks for God. All have turned aside; together they have become worthless; no one does good, not even one.*

[4] 1 John 4:16: *God is love, and whoever abides in love abides in God...*

[5] 1 Peter 5:10: *The God of all grace... will himself restore, confirm, strengthen, and establish you.*

[6] 1 Peter 3:18: *For Christ also suffered once for sins, the righteous for the unrighteous, that he might bring us to God.*

CHAPTER 5

HOW CAN I GET TO HEAVEN?

You are going to love this! You getting to heaven is a piece of cake. Jesus has literally done all of the hard work and the Holy Spirit will be doing all the heavy lifting. You don't even have to convince Father God to let you in—He wants you in!

Getting you saved so that you can get to heaven is your loving Father's idea from beginning to end. If the enemy had his way, you would never even realize that there is a heaven to go to (and a hell to avoid) and you would certainly never realize that you are going to need Jesus to save you in order to get you there.

God has been working to save you all throughout your life. You just may not be very aware of what He has been doing. So relax. You don't need to talk God into saving you or impress Him with how terrified you are of hell or how aghast you are at your own sinfulness. If you even have a glimmer of these realities, it is because He has been helping you to know the truth so that He can use your love of the truth (which He gives you) to save you.[1]

All you need to do to get to heaven is to "get saved." This phrase has many true facets of meaning which you will hear from time to time, such as "entering into a life-saving relationship with Jesus Christ"; "giving your life to Christ"; "having your sins forgiven"; "turning from sin to live for God"; "inviting Jesus into your heart and life"; "believing in what Jesus has done for you at the cross"; and of course "being born again."

Don't let this confuse you! The main idea is that you are making an appeal to God to save you and you are choosing to put your belief and trust in what He says He has done for you through Jesus Christ. This act of faith is our side of it in terms of the part we play.[2]

On the Father's side there is a lot going on that we can't see and only partially may feel or sense. These will be covered more fully in the chapter "What Is the New Birth?" For now let's just say that what is involved in our salvation is nothing less than making us entirely new creations placed in a new spiritual environment (new for us) called the Kingdom of God.[3] Truly, God does all of the hardest parts!

Preparing for the Steps

So far we have been talking about turning towards God to be saved so that we can get to heaven. This is the second half of salvation, so to speak, the longer and better half: Being saved *for God, for this life and for heaven*. The first part is being saved *from our sins and from hell*. The two go hand in hand. You absolutely cannot take sins with you into heaven. In fact they are guaranteed to take you in the opposite direction, if you cling to them down here!

These two sides of salvation are encompassed by a word which describes the necessary first step of the process: repentance. Repentance indicates a change of mind or a change of direction. It also carries a dual meaning: turning *from* sin and turning *towards* God. Repentance may include feeling sorry, but in essence it is a turning around. Imagine a traveler feeling sorry he is going in the wrong direction, but continuing on anyway—that's not repentance. Repentance is turning completely around and going the right way!

Desiring to be saved means, therefore, that there is a genuine willingness to give up *anything* in your life in order to turn to God. No one can become free of sin without God's help, so a part of repentance and the salvation which follows it, is seeking God's love, wisdom and power for complete deliverance from known sins. Fortunately for all of us, the Lord doesn't say, "Get free of your sins, and then I'll see about saving you." Mercifully, He receives all who turn to Him, no matter what their condition. Even so, there has to be a resolute and real decision to turn from sin as part of the turning to God. Otherwise, we are still heading the wrong way on the road, but praying that God will miraculously make it end at the right destination anyway. That's not being real!

What do you have to part with immediately? You have to give up at least those portions of pride and fear that have been holding you back. These may seem like friends and wise counselors, but they are not. Pride and fear are our enemies! They have pushed and pulled us into countless dangers and wrong directions. All along they have been thwarting God's desire to draw us into His loving embrace.

Don't worry; you don't have to give up *all* your pride and fear—even if you could. Alas, there is simply too much of it to become free all at once. Genuine liberation from those two formidable foes will take God working with us step by step as we get to know Him better. So, be prepared: You will have pride and fear dogging your steps for some time to come. This isn't a final farewell to those false friends, but it is a good beginning.

You would also be wise to give up your claim to yourself, your right to do things "my way." I have known many people who have been saved without doing this, but they are a sad sight, really. Trying to go on living for that false god Self with Jesus on the inside is an idea that cannot fly! What works beautifully is learning how to live for Jesus, allowing Him to take the lead. He knows what's truly good for you and always has your best at heart.

Why not give yourself fully and freely to Jesus and be done with it? Your life won't be worth a plugged nickel to you if you die without giving it to the Lord for Him to save. And it isn't worth much even now if you try to live without Him. It will never bring you peace and fulfillment unless it is given *entirely* to God. Don't wait to get to heaven to finally live for Jesus. Don't wait until you die to start living the heavenly life. It is meant to be lived down here!

> **But seek first the kingdom of God and his righteousness, and all these things will be added to you.** Matthew 6:33

The Steps to Heaven

The way up first leads us down. These steps to heaven begin by leading "downward" into the humility of total honesty, into facing unpleasant realities and into recognizing our moral failure.

Step 1. Realize that you *will* die one day. This first step to awakening is obvious once you have taken it. Nevertheless, countless multitudes live in apparent denial, thinking or hoping that they will never have to face the day of their own death. The truth is it won't kill you to look death square in the face—even your own inevitable death—nor will it rob you of your zest for life. And if things go well, you will arrive at the Right Solution to the death dilemma and a sword that has been hanging over your head will have been removed. That's a good thing![4] So, let's turn and face the dread reality: Every life ends in death. Or does it?

Step 2. Realize that you want to go to heaven, not hell. Life doesn't "just end" with death; it goes on long we die. Most of us have a nagging suspicion that there are only two possible outcomes to life on earth: eternal life or eternal death; eternal reward or eternal punishment; heaven or hell. No one wants to burn. Sure, some crazy, hell-bent rock stars think it's going to be a party down under, but no sane person believes that.

Step 3. Realize you can't get to heaven by yourself. You are doing great so far! You have passed two fundamental measures of sanity: a) you know you are not god and that your life on earth will end one day and b) you have the good sense to realize that you need to strap on a golden parachute before your plane crashes and burns. But that thought of burning forces to the surface the most troubling questions of all: "Do I qualify for heaven? Will God let me in? Why would God let me in?"

You may try to answer these questions with bluff and bluster: "I'm really not so bad. I'm certainly not as bad as others are, or as I could have been." Ah, yes, you have been *trying* to be good, but have you been good enough? Your conscience will never let you say that you have fully measured up to even your own (low) standards, much less God's.[5]

Step 4. Realize that you need someone to save you. It may hurt to admit it, but none of us have the power to rise to heaven on our own, nor do any of us have the moral character to qualify us for being raised up there by God. But don't think that all is lost! There is Someone who wants to save us; Someone who has the power to get us there; Someone who can "bend the rules" so that we can be allowed to enter in His Name is Jesus Christ and He is fully empowered and qualified by Father God to get anyone to heaven who wants to be saved by Him.[6] So, what are you waiting for? Take the next step!

5. Step 5. Go to that "Someone" and get saved!

Prayer

Father, my eyes are open! I can see that I am going to die one day and I sure don't want to end up in the wrong place. But I have to admit that I don't have the moral purity and perfection to be assured of making it to heaven on my own.

Thank You for seeing my need of Your saving help long before I did! Thank You for making me aware of an even greater need and desire—to know You. Please don't let me "sleep walk" through the rest of my life, missing out on the greatest gift life has to offer, a living, loving relationship with my God! Lead me now into the steps I need to take and the prayers I need to make. I am ready to give myself to You!

---

[1] 2 Thessalonians 2:13-14: *Because God chose you as the firstfruits to be saved, through sanctification by the Spirit and belief in the truth.*

[2] "Getting saved" is the essential first step into eternal life and it is incredibly easy; *staying* saved will come later. Wait for Chapter 13.

[3] 2 Corinthians 5:17: *Therefore, if anyone is in Christ, he is a new creation. The old has passed away; behold, the new has come;* Colossians 1:13-14: *He has delivered us from the domain of darkness and transferred us to the kingdom of his beloved Son.*

[4] King Solomon advised us all to gain wisdom by facing death: Ecclesiastes 7:4 AMP: *The heart of the wise is in the house of mourning, but the heart of fools is in the house of mirth and sensual joy.*

[5] Romans 3:23; previously cited, endnotes for Chapter 3.

[6] Peter, who was an eye-witness of the resurrection, declared Jesus to be the Savior of the whole world: Acts 4:11-12: *"This Jesus is the stone that was rejected by you, the builders, which has become the cornerstone. And there is salvation in no one else, for there is no other name under heaven given among men by which we must be saved."*

CHAPTER 6

HOW CAN I GET SAVED?

God has not made this hard for us! The only really difficult part is coming to the realization that we need God to save us. That usually means getting ourselves into terrible trouble or discovering what an undeniable moral failure we actually are. We may prolong the agony of self-discovery by thinking that we can fix our troubles (but we can't fix them all) and that we can fix our moral failures (but how can Self fix self?).[1]

We may hold out to our very last spiritual breath thinking "all is lost" or "I just can't give in," but if we are ready to reach out to God, the rest is easy. Jesus did the really hard part on the cross when He took the punishment our sins deserved. His "work" of dying for our sins is actually what gets us saved.[2] God wants this more than you do! So, put your doubts and fears aside as well as you can and let's go forward. The Lord knows how to meet you along the way. Just allow yourself to follow these simple steps, study the scriptures and say the prayers:

Steps to Salvation

Step 1. Admit you need God. Have you realized that your life is not working out—that it is going in the wrong direction? Have you realized that you cannot "fix" you and that no one else and nothing else can either? Good! Then what you have been going through has been teaching you a life-saving lesson! Now, you are ready to begin your true life.[3]

Step 2. Turn to God. This means turning all the way around: Away from your wrong ways and towards God and His ways. You have been showing Him your back; it's time to show Him your face and to start seeking to look in His face.[4]

Step 3. Confess to God. This is telling the truth to God, hiding nothing. The problem isn't other people, or the world God made, or God and His ways. It's you and your ways! Let Him know how you have lived for yourself and not for Him. Be honest with Him about how that has hurt others and yourself. Then "confess" your need of His mercy and help.[5]

Step 4. Believe in God. By an act of your will choose to believe that God really does love you, forgives you, and wants to save you through what Jesus has done for you at the cross. Now ask Jesus to come into your heart, into your life and to live His life in you. He is certain to do it! Be sure to say the prayers at the end of this chapter.

There Is So Much More

Now that you have prayed to be saved, you are! You may be feeling Christ's peace, fresh confidence or a sense of hope restored. You may have received a vision, felt His love or were touched by His presence. Or He may be asking you to simply take it on faith and just rest in that. The experience is different for everyone. The common element that dawns inside all of us is a faith-knowing, summed up in the phrase, "I know that I know that Jesus is alive!" and the willingness to declare that He is Lord.

If you confess with your mouth that Jesus is Lord and believe in your heart that God raised him from the dead, you will be saved. Romans 10:9

You will certainly want to "nail this down" by going to "How Can I Be Sure I'm Saved?" There is actually so much that has just taken place that it really needs a whole chapter to describe the birth that you have undergone ("What Is The New Birth?") and another to describe the life that you have now entered ("What Are My First Steps?'). Please keep reading!

Prayers

Father, please forgive me for all the ways in which I have lived for myself, hurt others, and turned my back on You. I confess and repent of all these sins. Thank You for loving me and making a way for my sins to be forgiven through Jesus.

Jesus, please come into my heart, into my life and live Your life in me. I surrender myself to You, body, soul and spirit. Grant me an assurance of my eventual entry into heaven won for me by Your death and resurrection. Help me by Your Word and Holy Spirit to trust and follow You step by step into the new life here on earth that You have also promised can be mine.

Holy Spirit, please come and heal my broken heart of all the hurt that my own sins and those of others have caused.

Show me and tell me Your truth in ways that I can receive and understand. Help me fight to remain loyal to the One who laid down His life for me by laying down my "old life" and my wrong ways for Him!

---

[1] Paul summarizes the human predicament with brutal honesty: Romans 7:18-19 AMP: *For I know that nothing good dwells within me, that is, in my flesh. I can will what is right, but I cannot perform it. [I have the intention and urge to do what is right, but no power to carry it out.] For I fail to practice the good deeds I desire to do, but the evil deeds that I do not desire to do are what I am [ever] doing.*

[2] Then, he answers his own heart cry and ours: Romans 7:24-25 AMP: *O unhappy and pitiable and wretched man that I am! Who will release and deliver me from [the shackles of] this body of death? O thank God! [He will!] through Jesus Christ (the Anointed one) our Lord!*

[3] Jesus is adamant that we cannot live without Him: John 15:4: *Abide in me, and I in you. As the branch cannot bear fruit by itself, unless it abides in the vine, neither can you, unless you abide in me.*

[4] Through Isaiah the Lord insists we turn to Him as the only way to be saved: Isaiah 45:22: *Turn to me and be saved, all the ends of the earth! For I am God, and there is no other;* Such repentance is not optional—not if we fear perishing: Luke 13:5: *Unless you repent, you will all likewise perish.*

[5] Hear the tender mercy of God making His appeal: Isaiah 1:18: *Come now, let us reason together, says the Lord: though your sins are like scarlet, they shall be as white as snow;* King David appealed to the Lord for mercy after murdering Uriah: Psalm 51:1: *Have mercy on me, O God, according to your steadfast love; according to your abundant mercy blot out my transgressions.*

CHAPTER 7

WHAT IS THE NEW BIRTH?

If you just prayed the prayers for how to get saved, you may be wondering, "What just happened to me?" That's a great question and it would take a lot more words on my part and will take a lot of living on your part to do justice to it. Like a young child you will be experiencing a true awaking of curiosity, especially in terms of the divine things which extend endlessly into the vast Mystery of God. You are now a learner for life! Your best teachers for this are the Word (Jesus) and the Holy Spirit.[1] All a primer like this can do is give you pointers. For instance, you have probably heard that being saved means being born again. But what does that mean?

Major Elements of the New Birth

The Lord has packed a lot into His answer to our prayer for salvation. You have been spiritually reborn— raised to new life by faith in Jesus Christ and by the gift of the Holy Spirit. It would be very easy to miss most of it and only go with the few things you may have felt or been shown. Here are some of the main items that may have escaped your notice:[2]

1) You were spiritually dead. Did you even know that? I sure didn't! In the moment of conversion God brought your spirit to life by putting His Spirit within you and reconnecting you with Himself.[3]

2) You have been sealed to God. Your spirit was joined to the Holy Spirit who came to live within you as a "guarantee" of good things to come.[4]

3) You received a heart transplant. The heart you had was self-centered, deceitful and corrupt in God's eyes, so He also placed a new heart within you. This heart is entirely good, just like that of Jesus.[5]

4) You were dead in your trespasses and sins. That's how deep the separation from God had become. Through your faith in Christ, God was fully able to cover your sins and cleanse you with the Blood that Jesus shed on your behalf.[6]

5) You have been "justified." God not only forgave you your sins, He also separated you from them. This is called justification. Because of your faith in Jesus, you have been given a standing or status with God that you don't deserve and could never earn. He has chosen to treat you with high favor, just as if you were a sinless child in His eyes.[7] You may indeed have sin in you, but you are not your sins!

6) You have been liberated. You were under the oppression of an invisible kingdom. You may have thought you were simply living on earth, but you were also held in bondage spiritually under the power and control of an invisible enemy operating in another realm contiguous with earth. In the moment of conversion, you were translated out of the kingdom of darkness and into the Kingdom of God's beloved Son.[8]

7) You were blind. There was a veil over your heart that obstructed your mind and kept you from "seeing" the resurrected Lord of all creation, Jesus Christ. That veil has been removed, allowing you to see Christ with eyes of faith. The eye of your heart has been enlightened and your lost spiritual sight has been restored.[9]

8) The Image of God has been restored to you. You had been created to both carry and reflect God's Image, but you had lost the vision. Now that His true Image has been restored to you as you behold God in the face of Jesus Christ, you are able to carry His Image in your heart and more truly reflect His Image by your life. This is what transforms you.[10]

9) You have been "reborn" as a new creation. *All* things have passed away; many new things have come.[11] You will still have plenty of your old ways, thoughts and feelings left to deal with—these haven't been eliminated—but you have been given a new power to overcome them.

10) You are now a child of God in the family of God. You were isolated from the family of faith, but now you have been adopted, "brought near" and made a member of Christ's Body on earth and in heaven.[12]

11) Get your space suit on for this one. You have been raised and are now seated with Christ in heavenly places. Clearly this is spiritual, not physical, however that doesn't mean it is any less

real. A part of you is seated with Christ, sharing in His authority.[13]

12) You are "in Christ" and He is in you. Your new life will only work properly as you trust yourself entirely to His love and leadership. As you trust and obey, He leads you into the life you both desire.[14]

Believe it or not, there's more! The gifts of God are too numerous to enumerate, which makes searching things out in His Word an adventure. Walking with God is like a treasure hunt with the clues scattered all over scripture.

The New Birth Compared to the First Birth

Jesus compared salvation directly to the birth process, telling Nicodemus that he "must be born again."[15] We have just surveyed a dozen different features of the new birth explained to us in the Bible. Now let's take up the birth metaphor itself and see what it can show us. When you were born the first time, who did most of the work—you, your parents, or God?

1. God gave you life through the seed of your father. However, your father didn't know you, only God did. Had it not been for God wanting to create you and choosing to bring you forth, you would have remained a gleam in your father's eye.

2. God shaped you in your mother's womb as her body nourished and grew you. However, your

mother didn't know you, only God did. Had it not been for God "forming" you in the hidden places and choosing to protect the growth of the life He placed within your mother, you would never have seen the light of day.

You did precisely nothing! At most we could say you willingly submitted to the process of being born, but even that is a stretch. What choice did you have? Your mother and father, on the other hand, made a real contribution. They were willing to do their part, but no one has the power to create life except God. The God of Life had to do all the hard, impossible things. Remember our "salvation basics"? Even our natural life was a gift of grace that we received (entered into, made use of, and enjoyed) "by faith", by entrusting ourselves to it.[16] Spiritual birth is very similar.

1. Like a father, God has been sowing His seeds of truth into "the womb" of your interior world (*seed* is the root word that *semen* comes from). He has used many people, some in positions of authority, to speak truth into your life. Don't just think Bible truths: All truth comes from God and can lead back to Him.[17]

2. Others, meanwhile, have been praying for your salvation. Like a mother the church has been welcoming and nurturing your life in Christ. God has used many believers' prayers to cultivate the words others have planted.

Once again, God does the impossible parts. All words, no matter how true, and all prayers, no matter how earnest, would accomplish nothing in terms of your salvation, unless it were God's good pleasure and free choice to bring you forth from your darkness into the light of His unending Day. In the hidden places deep within you the Holy Spirit has been wrestling with you through your conscience, working with the prayers He has gathered to bring those words to fruition. You have been "born again" by the most essential seed of them all—*by the implanted Word*!

> **Love one another earnestly from a pure heart, since you have been born again, not of perishable seed but of imperishable, through the living and abiding word of God.** 1 Peter 1:22-23

Compared to what God has done in saving us, compared to the ways He worked through others and all that they contributed, what have we done to accomplish our new birth? Precisely nothing! At most we could say we willingly submitted to the process of being born again, but even that is a stretch. What choice did we have? Like the "godfather" of movie fame, the One True Father "made us an offer we couldn't refuse!" He offered us life and we said "yes" to Jesus. Yet, even there, He had to work inside of us to make us willing to say yes. This is why God rightly gets *all* the glory and *all* the praise: We have been saved by God and His grace through faith, not of our own works.

Being Born Verses Being in the Womb

We compared being born again with natural birth the first time around. Now, let's look at the new birth as the successful completion of a birthing process by comparing life in the womb to life outside the womb. When Jesus spoke to Nicodemus about the necessity of being "born again", He wasn't denying the greatness of natural life, but indicating that natural life has very real limitations.[18] What is needed for our spiritual growth to take place is the kind of radical change that birth brings. This analogy invites us to compare the new birth to the experience of a child emerging from the womb.

The child is alive in the womb, but birth brings life-enhancing transformations in almost every way. Think for a moment about what that child might have been experiencing. Life in the womb wasn't so bad. Sure it was dark, a bit cramped and there was little real freedom to move about as you pleased, but it was safe, warm and very cozy. The world outside only penetrated with bumps, muffled sounds and vague impressions of light. It was easy to do nothing but sleep, stretch and drool. Then comes the big day: Contractions! Water break! Pressure and pushing! "What's happening to me?" Being born is a scary, painful process! It is also an irreversible "step" into a great unknown.

After going through many changes the new born child emerges into a wonder-filled environment at a level of life it could never have reached on its own. It has been a journey from darkness into light, from isolation into family, from restraint into freedom, and

41

from helpless dependence into ever increasing abilities and independence. In the womb the child was entirely self-centered; after the womb the child grows into a vital relationship with the ones who gave it life. In the womb the infant knew practically nothing; after the womb the real learning begins. In the womb the fetus was loved; after the womb the baby can begin to love in return.

It only takes a little imagination to compare our natural birth to the superior realities and enhanced relationships that are associated with our spiritual rebirth!

Prayer

Father, thank You! I had no idea that You would be doing so much for me! Help me to grow in knowing how great Your salvation truly is. Help me stay grateful for all that You are doing to save me for heaven and to bring heaven's way of life into my life now.

---

[1] Jesus is known to us as both the Eternal Word and the Living Word: John 1:1-2, 14: *In the beginning was the Word, and the Word was with God, and the Word was God. He was in the beginning with God;* The Holy Spirit is our Teacher: John 14:26: *But the Helper, the Holy Spirit… will teach you all things and bring to your remembrance all that I have said to you.*

[2] Titus 3:4- AMP: *He saved us, not because of any works of righteousness that we had done, but because of His own pity and mercy, by [the] cleansing [bath] of the new birth (regeneration) and renewing of the Holy Spirit.*

[3] This is called regeneration and it is God's answer to the spiritual death which came on all of us due to Adam's sin: Ezekiel 11:19: *And I will give them one heart, and a new spirit I will put within them.*

---

⁴ Ephesians 1:13-14: *In him you also… were sealed with the promised Holy Spirit, who is the guarantee of our inheritance until we acquire possession of it.*

⁵ Ezekiel 11:19; previously cited. Be on guard, however: The old heart still lurks in the shadows, seeking to overthrow you in a heartbeat.

⁶ Although our former condition of spiritual death (due to Adam's sin) was not our fault, we are responsible for the spiritual death our own sins produced in us: Ephesians 2:1-2: *And you were dead in the trespasses and sins in which you once walked*; God's solution is the Blood of Christ: Ephesians 1:7-8: *In him we have redemption through his blood, the forgiveness of our trespasses.*

⁷ Romans 3:22-24: *For there is no distinction: for all… are justified by his grace as a gift, through the redemption that is in Christ Jesus.*

⁸ Colossians 1:13-14: *He has delivered us from the domain of darkness and transferred us to the kingdom of his beloved Son.*

⁹ The most important truth about our universe is that it is centered in Jesus Christ, our Creator, Savior and Lord. Yet neither science nor reason can probe this FACT for it is hidden from us by an invisible enemy due to Adam's sin: 2 Corinthians 4:3-6: *And even if our gospel is veiled, it is veiled only to those who are perishing. In their case the god of this world has blinded the minds of the unbelievers…*

¹⁰ Will power and good intentions cannot change you. Only this: 2 Corinthians 3:18: *And we all, with unveiled face, beholding the glory of the Lord, are being transformed into the same image…*

¹¹ 2 Corinthians 5:17-18: *Therefore, if anyone is in Christ, he is a new creation. The old has passed away; behold, the new has come.*

¹² Ephesians 2:13, 19: *You are fellow citizens with the saints and members of the household of God.*

¹³ Ephesians 2:6: *Seated us with him in the heavenly places in Christ Jesus.*

¹⁴ Galatians 2:20: *I have been crucified with Christ…*

¹⁵ Notice that Jesus doesn't consider the new birth to be optional: John 3:7: *Do not marvel that I said to you, 'You must be born again.'*

¹⁶ Jesus compared the trusting way that children approach the gift of natural life, to the way we are meant to enter spiritual life: Mark 10:15-16: *Whoever does not receive the kingdom of God like a child shall not enter it.*

¹⁷ Jesus didn't just tell us truth; He claimed to *be* truth John 14:6: *Jesus said to him, "I am the way, and the truth, and the life."*

¹⁸ Notice the progression: Seeing is followed by entering the kingdom, then living the life of the kingdom as free as a leaf in the wind: John 3:3-8: *Unless one is born again he cannot see the kingdom of God… unless one is born of water and the Spirit, he cannot enter the kingdom of God… The wind blows where it wishes, and you hear its sound, but you do not know where it comes from or where it goes. So it is with everyone who is born of the Spirit.*

CHAPTER 8

HOW DOES GOD SAVE ME?

We are saved by grace through faith! This is the mighty "formula" which God has worked out for our salvation. He has been doing this every moment of your life, though you probably didn't know it, and will continue doing this all through eternity.

> **For by grace you have been saved through faith, and that not of yourselves; it is the gift of God, not of works, that no one would boast.** Ephesians 2:8-9 WEB

This compact statement needs to be taken apart, so that we can truly grasp the two most important practical aspects of salvation: a) what God is doing for us and b) what is required of us to do. Here is the gospel of salvation in its simplicity:

1. "**Saved**" means two things: Getting you to heaven and getting heaven's way of life into you on earth. We all need to be saved, both down here and for up there. None of us can save ourselves. The "good news" is that God loves us, wants to save us and has made a way to do it through Jesus Christ.

2. "**By grace**" means that God's way of saving us is to give everything to us and do everything for us that we cannot do for ourselves (which is just about everything).[1] He is even helping us with the parts

45

that we need to do! Grace works for us, before us, with us and through us.

3. "Through faith" means that our part includes believing in and trusting in what God says He is doing and has done. This opens the way for the Spirit to work in us, helping us want to love the Lord and to follow His ways. We don't "work" our way to heaven; we "trust" our way there by the work God does through Jesus and by the Holy Spirit.

4. "Not of works" means that there is nothing we can do to earn or deserve this gift of God's grace and mercy. Not even our faith is a "work" that saves us. We trust in God's love, Jesus' work at the cross and the Spirit's power.

Never lose sight of these basics! You will need a "good grip" on grace in order to have a continuing confidence and joy in your salvation—the saving act that has already taken place which will bring you one day to heaven. You will also need a masterful grip on grace to stay surrendered to your Lord, live by His peace and flow in His Spirit, so that His salvation can also bring you into heaven's way of life on earth.

Since so much of the New Testament is devoted to explaining what it means to be saved and how that should impact the way that we live, this is by no means a small subject in scripture.[2] Plan on reading all that the Bible has to say, for we have an enemy, who tries in every conceivable way to obstruct or obscure the simple truth of the gospel and to rob it of its power.

By Grace through Faith Now and Forever

Throughout your very long life, which begins here and continues seamlessly into eternity, the great truth that you are being saved by grace through faith will never change. The only thing that will change is that you will begin to trust Jesus and yield yourself to God and His grace more and more, until you trust Him completely with everyone you love and everything you have to manage. In heaven you will be totally trusting that God will forever be supplying you life and all that a rich, full life requires. The tremendous "secret" is that God is *already* giving you *down here* everything that you need for life itself and for right living (which is heaven's way of life).[3]

You may be seeing clearly enough your need for God to save you, especially in terms of getting you to heaven. Don't let that entirely steal your focus! This is merely the entry point to a total transformation of the way you are meant to see the whole of life. Even so, this entry point is where we learn the liberating truth that God's work to save us for heaven is based on His grace and is received by us through our faith. However, our need is far in excess of simply getting to heaven when we die. Everything about us needs saving if we are ever to be raised *in this life* into the "glorious liberty" of the children of God, living heaven's way of life while still on earth.[4]

By God's design, your way of entry into that process of growth will soon turn your attention from eternal salvation (as you become more confident of it) to the more mundane earthly needs you have for God, now

47

that you know that He is real and that He wants to save you. Not knowing God until we are finally "saved" means that we haven't been consciously aware of what is available to us from God. Our true education can't begin until we meet the Teacher! Naturally, the Lord will go to work to make every new believer aware of how much they need God and how much He makes available. This *always* means encountering problems and difficulties that you will need God's help with.[5]

Our two most obvious needs down here are for God's saving mercy and His saving help. God's mercy comes to us primarily through the gift of Jesus' death for us; God's help comes to us primarily through the gift of Holy Spirit's work for us. Just as Jesus died for us our death; Holy Spirit has come to be our new life. As we slowly learn to trust Jesus' death to be a full and sufficient covering for us whenever we sin and seek mercy again; so too we slowly learn to trust Holy Spirit's guidance into the new life of love and faithfulness that we yearn to live.

Due to the fall from grace we have a dual problem: We are bound by sin and we are blind to truth from God's perspective (the only one that counts). Because of our common weakness at overcoming sin in our own strength, you will have plenty of opportunities to go to God for mercy. Due to our common blindness of what is really right, good and true in each situation, you will have plenty of troubles you will need God's help in overcoming. These dual needs drive us all to God—if we let them—and it is there that we discover the way to overcome is by learning how to be saved by God's grace through faith time and time again.[6]

48

As this process takes place, the recognition of your sins will make you seek God as your Savior, both in terms of forgiveness for having sinned, and for help in overcoming them. We could say that this first stage is learning to get sin out; the second stage is learning to get more of Jesus in! This process of repenting of sins and seeking mercy and help will greatly grow your appreciation of God's love, patience, mercy and grace, which you will need as you turn towards the higher calling of living by His Spirit.

The Choice That Is Ever Before You

You will need God's help learning how to live in His peace, confidence and joy when you are besieged by problems. This is by no means easy at first, because our trust levels in God are so low. His answer, however, is always the same: "Trust Me and obey Me." Jesus hasn't saved you for heaven so that you can live your life any way you want to on earth. He has saved you by introducing you to Himself, so that now you can trust and follow Him as He leads you step by step into what He has planned for you.

Just like those first disciples, you have a choice now that you have met Jesus. Will you "go back to your nets," or will you leave everything to follow Him? If you try to cling to your life, keeping everything under your preferences and control, He says that you will lose your life for sure![7] The only way forward is to seek to follow Him. He wants to lead you into life. He is the only one who can do it. *Apart from Him* you can no sooner enjoy heaven's way of living down here, than

49

you can mount up in your own strength to gain it up there. We are meant to open our hearts to Jesus the way a flower opens to sunshine.

The first step with Jesus is always to trust Him with everything and anything that has just happened. The second is to seek Him so that you can handle things His way. As the trusting grows, the obedience becomes easier and more natural, because our desire to do the next right thing is supernaturally sustained by the Holy Spirit whenever our hearts are fully surrendered to the Lord. Learn these prayers and make them your favorite travelling companions: "Jesus, what do You want me to do next? What are You trying to show me? How should I respond to this situation?" Trust, listen and obey.

As you learn to trust your own life to Jesus, He will begin helping you learn how to trust your loved ones to Him as well: First, that He will get them to heaven; second, that He will help them with every other concern you may have for their well being. In this way we learn by a natural grace to become intercessors for those we already love.

Beyond this, is becoming so enamored with Jesus that you begin to care for the ones He loves that perhaps you haven't: the hurt, the lost, the needy, the lonely, the sinful, and the forgotten ones. In short, everybody else! He will show you some of the ways He wants to save them through your prayers, your words and your work. Then He will help you to trust Him to work through you as you trust, listen and obey.

Nobody walks this path perfectly, so don't be discouraged at the sight of it. I wanted you to see a wider perspective on God's work in your life, not so that you would begin doing all of these things right away, but in order for you to understand how absolutely pervasive the working of God's salvation truly is. And it is all based on this one perfect "formula": We are saved by grace through faith.

You Lived by Grace Once Before

It may surprise you to know that God has always been working in your life, saving you by grace through faith. When you were a little child, it was the grace of God's Spirit working with you, helping you to explore your world, teaching you how to laugh, learn, love and play. The Spirit is so good at doing this without calling attention to Himself that you never knew your life was being sustained by the superabundance of God's saving gifts.[8] One of those key gifts is the provision of a trusting nature to little children: Without it the child could receive nothing! Indeed, the telling sign of a lost childhood is the inability to be as trusting as a little child. Jesus says that unless we become childlike again (with His help), we will by no means enter the Kingdom He desires to bring into our lives down here.[9]

Even things that we typically pride ourselves for are His saving gifts: intelligence, common sense, outward beauty, physical strength, family and national heritage. If we step back a bit, we can easily see that no one can give these things to themselves! God is the giver—that's what grace means. OK, but what about things our efforts have made of these "starter kits"? Surely, we "gave" ourselves things that we have worked hard for: character, virtues, educational degrees, occupational success, material prosperity, etc. Once again, if you step

51

back far enough, you would have to admit that something in you made you want to work hard, providing the desire and motivation to build upon what you were originally given. That "something" is a gift of grace which has "saved" you in these dimensions of accomplishment. This is not to belittle your part but to help you magnify God's. In this way you will gain eyes to see how to entrust everything in your life to the God who has already been bringing life to you.

Can you see by this how utterly pervasive God's giving of everything necessary for life and right living truly has been in your life? Every good gift comes from the Father of Lights and it has power to "save" us from the deprivation, destruction or darkness it's absence would allow.[10] There is far more to your salvation than simply getting you to heaven! In the next three chapters we will explore further what these key concepts of salvation, grace and faith mean for us.

Prayers

Father, I have spent my whole life trying to save myself in one situation after another. Now, at last I'm beginning to see that You have been wanting to be my Savior all along. You want to save me by getting me to heaven through what Jesus has done for me. And You want to save me in every situation and circumstance of my life—no matter how badly I'm doing or how difficult it is. I gladly accept Your gift of grace! Help me to believe in You and all You are doing for me through Jesus and by Your Spirit.

Jesus, thank You for doing the work I would never have been able to do, in going to the cross for me. Thank You for saving me from the hell my sins deserved! Thank You for making a way to for me to enjoy eternal life with You in heaven! Help me now to learn how to live in this life by trusting You and following You. I desire to become Your heaven-directed and Spirit-filled servant and friend.

Holy Spirit, I am going to need a lot of help from You to keep me in remembrance that it is not me who saves me, but God and Jesus. Forgive me for grieving You so often in the past by not listening to Your voice in my conscience. Help me learn to listen to You now! Grow my eyes to see and my ears to hear everything You are speaking to me and showing me in the Word and in the world.

---

[1] Now that you know Jesus, our Father is giving you everything you need to live fully and to live rightly; our task is to learn to live by what He supplies: 2 Peter 1:3: *His divine power has granted to us all things that pertain to life and godliness.*

[2] See especially Romans 1-8, then all of Galatians and Ephesians.

[3] 2 Peter 1:3; previously cited.

[4] Romans 8:21 AMP: *That nature (creation) itself will... [gain an entrance] into the glorious freedom of God's children.*

[5] According to Jesus troubles are "guaranteed" to come your way, so be prepared: John 16:33: *In the world you will have tribulation. But take heart; I have overcome the world.*

[6] By "looking" the Lord means focusing upon Him, not the problem; then trust Him, follow Him and the salvation will surely come: Isaiah 45:22 AMP: *Look to Me and be saved, all the ends of the earth!*

[7] Matthew 16:24-25: *For whoever would save his life will lose it, but whoever loses his life for my sake will find it.*

[8] See John 16 and Acts 2 for more on the Holy Spirit.

[9] Jesus word here about entering the kingdom of heaven applies to heaven's reign *on earth*. "Saving faith" gets us into heaven in the next life, but childlike trust is required for entering into a heavenly life in this life. Matthew 18:3 AMP: *Unless you repent (change, turn about) and become like little children... you can never enter the kingdom of heaven [at all].*

[10] James 1:17: *Every good gift and every perfect gift is from above, coming down from the Father of lights.*

CHAPTER 9

WHAT IS SALVATION?

Why did you want to be saved? Some people seek Jesus as a way of getting to heaven. They want to be saved from hell: from the fear of death or from the fear of punishment. Others seek Him to be saved from some form of hell on earth: from the pain of a lost love one, or a failed career, or fears, or depression, or weaknesses. A few may possibly come to Jesus just wanting to be saved from not knowing the Beautiful God who created them. *All of these are great reasons for wanting to be saved!*

If you are reading this, hopefully one of those reasons has already prompted you to seek Jesus for salvation. (If not, do it now! Follow the prayer steps in "How can I be saved?") But being saved and feeling the joy of it—as terrific as that is—is just the beginning of a saving embrace that goes on into all of eternity. Listen to this passage from the New Testament:

Consequently, he is able to save to the uttermost those who draw near to God through him, since he always lives to make intercession for them. Hebrews 7:25

Being saved "to the uttermost" is a very wide word indeed. It covers everything about us that needs rescue, repair, restoration or refreshing. As great as our need is, our God's salvation is even greater. Never imagine that "being saved" means that you have no further need of God to save you. *Don't put this in the past tense!* You are in a process of being saved from *all* that is not heavenly.

You definitely need Jesus to save you from your sins so that you have a hope of heaven; but you will also need Jesus to save you from yourself—so that He can get His heavenly life into you down here.[1]

Think of it: You are being saved from all that is not heavenly in your heart, mind, soul and body.[2] Of course the fullness of salvation in all of these areas won't come until you enter into the direct presence of Jesus after death. But it is going on now! And the world around you is also in a process of being saved from all that it, too, has fallen into of spiritual darkness and material decay.[3] God is at work to rescue, repair, restore and renew the entire earth. True, the final outworking of the earth's salvation will require Jesus to come personally and take direct charge of the process. But *His Kingdom has already started the invasion!*

> **Pray then like this: "Our Father in heaven, hallowed be your name. Your kingdom come, your will be done, on earth as it is in heaven."** Matthew 6:9-10

Prayer

Father, You're right! I don't just need Your salvation to get me to heaven. I need You to be saving me in all kinds of ways here on earth. For starters please begin saving all of my loved ones. Bring them to know Jesus, too! I also need Your help in all my relationships. Save me from being selfish and self-centered, from taking more than giving, from hurting more than helping, and from hating rather than loving. While you are at, go to work on all of my attitudes and ways that don't match up with how Jesus in me wants me to live. As I learn to trust and obey Jesus, send Your salvation into every area of my life. Especially save me from living for myself, rather than for Jesus. May Your Kingdom come!

---

[1] On the need for being rescued from self-rule, see Jesus' teaching on the disciple's cross, repeated three times in the gospels (Matthew 16:24; Mark 8:34; Luke 9:23): Matthew 16:24-25: *If anyone would come after me, let him deny himself and take up his cross and follow me.*

[2] How complete and far-reaching will the Lord's salvation become in your life? Don't set any limits to it! Go for the gold: 1 Thessalonians 5:23: *Now may the God of peace himself sanctify you completely, and may your whole spirit and soul and body be kept blameless...*

[3] The vision that has always stirred me (as a former hippie and nature lover) is that our "glorious liberty" and creation's are intertwined. Let's go for this: Romans 8:20-21: *For the creation was subjected to futility, not willingly, but because of him who subjected it, in hope that the creation itself will be set free from its bondage to decay and obtain the freedom of the glory of the children of God.*

CHAPTER 10

WHAT IS GRACE?

Grace is the unexpected miracle of forgiveness and new life which saves us. The story goes that C. S. Lewis, a much beloved Christian writer of the last century, was once passing by a conference on comparative religions at Oxford where the issue being debated was what belief, if any, was unique to Christianity. On hearing the topic he said, "Oh that's easy. It's grace!"[1]

For by grace you have been saved through faith, and that not of yourselves; it is the gift of God, not of works, that no one would boast. Ephesians 2:8-9 WEB

Grace is the unexpected answer that God gives us to all our problems. Grace is unexpected because it is so entirely undeserved. When considering our sins and sinfulness, what we actually deserve from God are reprimands, reproaches, even punishments. But He shows us love and mercy instead. When we fail, He gives help and wisdom without the slightest trace of ill will. Grace is just the reverse from what we might expect: It is a living, flowing torrent of blessing.[2]

Grace is unnatural; it seems "out of order." We are not accustomed to finding it in our dealings with each other, so God's lavish use of it takes us by surprise. In our world "what goes around comes around." The rule of relationships is "I'll scratch your back, if you scratch mine." The rule of trade is "You get what you pay for." The rule of success is "If you want it, you'll have to work hard for it." But grace gives without any expectation of return. Grace gives first.[3] Grace keeps giving. Grace takes great joy in giving.

Grace is vast! Grace is so much more than a blessing spoken over meals. It is also (incredibly) so much more than what Jesus did for us on the cross. How could anything top that? Actually, something does. The Father's love is a grace given to us—a completely undeserved, life-giving blessing. Had the Father not loved us even when we were weak, even when we were enemies, even when we were ungodly, even when we were sinners, Jesus would never have been asked to die for us.[4]

Grace, therefore, begins with the Father of Lights, who is the Giver of every good gift.[5] Grace actually means "gift": Every gift is a grace bestowed upon us, a good thing freely given to us by the Father. "Saving grace" simply signifies those specific gifts from God that we need to save us.

Grace is universal. We may not encounter it very often where we live—in the midst of our self-centered inner life or our daily relationships in the world—but grace is the stuff the universe is made of. God made everything out of nothing. From the smallest life forms to the most gigantic stars, He not only made the universe functional, He also made it exquisitely beautiful. That is a colossal gift of grace! He didn't consult any of us before creating us and giving us a life by which to explore His beautiful world. That is a tender gift of grace. Nor did He wait for us to ask, but through conscience, dreams, right desires and high ideals He began leading us towards good things. That is an intimate gift of grace!

You Can Bet Your Life on Grace

Grace is indestructible! Since God is asking us to bet our lives on His grace always being there for us, He has shown us how powerful it is.

1. Grace is backed up by the very nature of God. God is the God of All Grace.[6] Giving grace may seem unnatural for us (hence we have a hard time trusting ourselves to it), but it comes naturally to God. It is the way He is. He is not about to change. *That's grace.*

2. Grace is backed up by the written promises of God. God knows that to us He's invisible. It isn't that He is truly invisible; it's just that we are blind. To help us He has given us the visible evidence of His Word. The Father has sworn by His own Word, Jesus has testified to the truth of the Word, and martyrs throughout the ages have given their lives in witness to the Word. *That's grace.*

3. Grace is demonstrated by the Blood of His Son. Before we even knew we needed mercy, God sent Jesus to the cross. The Blood Jesus shed is a vibrant demonstration of the Father's love and a visible proof (to our eyes of faith) that our sins have been fully covered.[7] *That's grace!*

4. Grace is guaranteed by the gift of the Spirit. The Holy Spirit has freely chosen in love to live within us. Not only that but He has volunteered to be

61

united to us as a guarantee of the good things to come, as sure and certain evidence that we are being saved.[8] All of the help He gives us is His gift of grace to us, whether it is comfort, joy, encouragement, understanding of the scriptures, love of the truth, hope, strength to persevere, correction, guidance or empowerment for ministry. *That's a whole lot of grace!*

Grace is not merely an attribute of God as great as that would be. Grace is a "code name" for the Father who loves us; Jesus whose Blood saves us; and the Spirit who helps us. Whenever you experience a moment saturated with grace, you have just had a close personal encounter with your God!

Prayer

Father, thank You for opening my eyes and helping me to see how gracious and giving You have always been. Thank You for the gift of life and love, forgiveness and mercy. Thank You for the gift of family and friends. Thank You for the gifts of talents, abilities and right desires. Thank You for all the ways You have been leading me by Your Holy Spirit. Above all thank You for the incomparable gift of Your Son Jesus Christ to be my Savior, Best Friend and Lord! Grant me one thing more: an ever grateful heart!

---

[1] This story was told by Philip Yancey in *What's so Amazing about Grace?* He attributed it to Scott Hoezee, *The Riddle of Grace*. Grand Rapids: Eerdmans, 1996, pg 42. There Hoezee attributed it to a speech given by

---

Peter Kreeft at Calvin College. Lewis' step-son Douglas Gresham mentioned in an interview with Max McLean that the remark actually took place during an impromptu discussion in a common room at Oxford (where Lewis was a professor). That's as far as the trail leads!

[2] Isaiah 64:4: *From of old no one has heard or perceived by the ear, no eye has seen a God besides you, who acts for those who wait for him.*

[3] He desires us first; He reaches out to us first; He came to us first: Isaiah 65:1-2: *I was ready to be sought by those who did not ask for me; I was ready to be found by those who did not seek me. I said, "Here am I, here am I," to a nation that was not called by my name. I spread out my hands all the day to a rebellious people, who walk in a way that is not good, following their own devices.*

[4] Romans 5:6-10; previously cited, endnotes for Chapter 4.

[5] Think about it: Every good thing that has ever come into your life had its origin in God's love for you! James 1:17: *Every good gift and every perfect gift is from above, coming down from the Father of lights.*

[6] 1 Peter 5:10: *The God of all grace, who has called you to his eternal glory...*

[7] 1 John 4:10-11: *In this is love, not that we have loved God but that he loved us and sent his Son to be the propitiation for our sins.*

[8] Ephesians 1:13-14: *In him you also... were sealed with the promised Holy Spirit, who is the guarantee of our inheritance...*

CHAPTER 11

WHAT IS FAITH?

Faith is not monolithic. Just as there is grace (what God does all the time) and there is "saving grace" (what God does specifically to help us become saved), there is faith (all manner of trust and belief) and "saving faith" (the ability to believe in what Jesus has done). Saving faith is different from other kinds of faith.

One huge difference is that *saving faith is a once and for all gift* to you of faith in Christ. It does not have to be grown. It is full and complete upon arrival![1] You would have been just as fully saved all the way to heaven, had you died the first day you were born again, as you will be saved even after a long season of fruitful service.

Once you "know that you know that you know" that Jesus is both Savior and Lord, you have received saving faith and there is no need to add anything to it in terms of your entry into heaven. Jesus did all the work to get you there and this is all that is needed for you to pass through the gates. Even so, you will certainly want to grow a powerful faith-confidence that you do indeed have saving faith. *Sounds like a paradox right?*

Let's put it this way: Even a brand new, untested and untried Christian has "saving faith" in that they now have put their belief in what Jesus has done for them and God has given them an assurance that Jesus is indeed their Savior and Lord. If they die tonight, they go straight to heaven! They have turned to God; they have opened their heart to God; they have trusted in Jesus to be their Savior; and God is fully satisfied.

You Will Be Tested On This

When the tests and trials come, however, each new Christian discovers how hard it is to keep believing with confidence and assurance that God is still fully committed to saving them. They discover instead the weakness of their faith and this usually causes them to question if they are really saved, or if they have sufficient faith to be saved. What we all have to learn is that it is not our faith that saves us. Faith is not the work that qualifies us for heaven. It is simply the way that God has given for us to receive the work He has done.[2]

This is why having saving faith and having confidence that we actually have saving faith are two separate issues. If you "know that you know that Jesus is Savior and Lord" you have saving faith![3] But are you always confident that faith in Christ alone is enough to save you? Do you always have peace that you are still being saved by God, no matter how badly you may be doing at the moment? Can you "reach through" the trial and take fresh hope and joy from confidence that "at least I'm going to heaven", despite your poor showing in the trial? These are the issues of growing confidence that the saving faith you've received is all you really need to get you to heaven.[4] Please see "How can I be sure I'm saved?" coming up next.

Try to keep in mind that we do *not* work in order to "get" God to save us for that is His unchanging desire. We "work" at believing His Word, at knowing Him and at trusting Him in order to more fully experience the joy of our salvation. Keeping our faith connection in good working order enables us to receive the benefits of what God desires to do for us by His grace.

This is just the first kind of faith-confidence that we need to cultivate. There are a lot of other kinds of faith to grow! There is *faith as intellectual belief* in the truths God reveals to your mind through His Word.[5] There is *faith as trust* in your heart that allows you to surrender fully to God, casting everything you care about and everyone you love upon Him to manage.[6] There is *faith as loyalty* to Jesus that enables you to follow Him even when He seems to be going in the exact opposite direction from your desires and even when the way is hard, dark and slippery.[7] These will take a lifetime of cultivation!

Beyond this there is faith for healing, faith for miracles, faith for answers to prayer, faith for risky steps of obedience.[8] These are not exactly separate categories, just handy ways of thinking and talking about the various ways faith operates and the areas of cultivation we may need to attend to.

The Place of Faith

Let's go over our God-given "formula" for salvation summarized for us in Paul's letter to the Ephesians:

For by grace you have been saved <u>through faith</u>, and that not of yourselves; it is the gift of God, not of works, that no one would boast. Ephesians 2:8-9 WEB

"By faith" means that our part includes believing in and trusting to what God says He is doing and has done. This opens the way for the Holy Spirit to work in us and through us, helping us want to love God and to follow His ways. We don't "work" our way to heaven; we "trust" our way there to the work God does through Jesus and through the Holy Spirit.

Now faith is the assurance of things hoped for, the conviction of things not seen. Hebrews 11:1

Prayer

Father, I am so grateful for the faith that You are giving me in the life, death and resurrection of Your Son Jesus Christ. In times like these I can feel it rising within me! Help me now to take that faith and spread it over all the situations in my life.

Jesus you are the Living Word. Grow within me a great faith in all of the truths of Your written Word. Help me feed on the scriptures and on Your faithfulness so that my faith can grow ever stronger. May You also grow my faith as I seek to become faithful at trusting and obeying You.

Holy Spirit I ask You to strengthen me to recognize, accept and believe all of the truths that You will be showing me in the Word, through my conscience and through my conversations with others. Convict and convince me of truth that I may become a person of true convictions.

---

[1] Romans 5:1-2: *Therefore, since we have been justified by faith, we have peace with God through our Lord Jesus Christ;* Galatians 3:11-12: *No one is justified before God by the law, for "The righteous shall live by faith."*

[2] This is the way of all human gift giving as well: One desires freely to give; the other merely trusts enough to *receive* what is given.

---

[3] Romans 10:9; previously cited, p. 33.

[4] Grow a strong "faith-grip" on grace: Hebrews 3:14: *For we share in Christ, if indeed we hold our original confidence firm to the end.*

[5] Hearing and believing scripture grows faith: Romans 10:17: *So faith comes from hearing, and hearing through the word of Christ.*

[6] Paul gives us the perfect picture of a surrendered and submitted heart: Galatians 2:20 AMP: *The life I now live in the body I live by faith in (by adherence to and reliance on and complete trust in) the Son of God, Who loved me and gave Himself up for me.*

[7] Real growth comes through hard trials: James 1:2-4: *Count it all joy, my brothers, when you meet trials of various kinds, for you know that the testing of your faith produces steadfastness.* (See also: Hebrews 6:11-12; 1 Peter 1:6-9)

[8] As an example of a faith that needs to be cultivated to be effective: Mark 11:22-24: *And Jesus answered them, "Have faith in God. Truly, I say to you, whoever says to this mountain, 'Be taken up and thrown into the sea,' and does not doubt in his heart, but believes that what he says will come to pass, it will be done for him."*

CHAPTER 12

HOW CAN I BE SURE I'M SAVED

What a tragedy it would be if we were to go through all of our life tormented by a secret fear that maybe we aren't really saved. The truth is no one ever deserves to be saved. No one ever lives fully worthy of salvation. Everyone has to be saved by the Blood of Jesus and the mercy and grace of God. Period.

Therefore no one can truly take any confidence about their salvation if they keep looking to themselves and checking to see how they are doing as a sign of whether or not they are going to be saved in the end. The only way to settle this issue and to finally and fully lay all fears to rest is to let God's Word declare the truth and then stand on it with believing faith, resisting all temptations to doubt what God has written.

Allow yourself to follow these simple steps, see what the scriptures say, then pray the prayers and take your stand. Don't be surprised if you have to stoutly resist some doubts and fears. Eventually, they will die down, vanquished by your faith in grace and in God's Word.

Steps to Confidence

Step 1. Make up your mind and settle it in your heart. As long as you look to your own weaknesses and failures you will find plenty of reasons to doubt that you are saved. But we are not saved by our "doing"—it is a free gift that we receive through our

71

believing! Choose to believe what God's Word says and stick with it. Since we are "saved by grace through faith," the critical question is this: "Do I have saving faith?"[1]

Step 2. Do you believe in Jesus? Jesus says that anyone who believes in Him shall not perish but have eternal life. We are saved because of what Jesus did for us, not anything we can do. Faith is how we receive the salvation God wants us to have.

> **"For God so loved the world, that he gave his only Son, that whoever believes in him should not perish but have eternal life."** John 3:16

Step 3. But do I really have *saving faith*? This is where many people get trapped by doubts. ("If I really believed wouldn't I be doing better? Why don't I feel it more?") Let the truth of scripture set you free: Paul clearly tells us what saving faith is. It is being able to state out loud that "Jesus is Lord" and to believe in our heart that He was raised from the dead. This is the "evidence" within us that we have received the gift of saving faith: We now know who Jesus is (as Lord of heaven and earth) and what He has done (as the Savior who died for our sins and was raised to life). Note well how absolute the promise is:

> **If you confess with your mouth that Jesus is Lord and believe in your heart that God raised him from the dead, you will be saved.** Romans 10:9

Step 4. Can I lose it? Not if you keep calling on His Name! Don't risk letting your faith fade away over time. Keep it "alive and well" by calling, asking, pleading for His help whenever you need help. The Lord promises to *always* save those who do. If we stay steadfast in calling on His Name, this scripture provides an unassailable confidence that our salvation has truly begun and is continuing.

> For "everyone who calls on the name of the Lord will be saved." Romans 10:13

A tripod is a remarkably stable construct. You can take a three-legged stool and place it firmly on any terrain. These three scriptures taken together will keep you standing solidly against any attempt by the enemy to put you off balance, doubting your salvation. I suggest that you memorize them, but at the very least, make sure you drink in deeply the saving truths they are telling you and know where to find them when you need them. Once the Lord showed me this "tripod" in scripture, my confidence and the joy of my salvation became very solidly seated in me indeed.[2]

Prayers

Father, please forgive me for doubting that You love me. I keep looking at my failures and many weaknesses and just can't see how You can. But You say that You sent Jesus to the cross out of love for me. I cast down all doubt and fear and choose to believe that You are not lying to me!

Jesus, please forgive me for doubting what You have done for me. You died on that cross for all of my sins and I know it! You have given me faith to believe it. Help me conquer my unbelief and live with confidence.

Holy Spirit, please come and help me take my stand once and for all on the truth, no matter what my feelings or other thoughts may be saying. I repent of looking to me (and how I'm doing) instead of to God and His Word!

---

[1] Ephesians 2:8; previously cited, endnotes for Chapter 2.

[2] Who is more joyful over your salvation: You or the God who is saving you? Psalm 51:12: *Restore to me the joy of your salvation, and uphold me with a willing spirit.*

CHAPTER 13

HOW CAN I STAY SAVED?

The key to staying saved is staying connected to Jesus! This should be evident, since it is Jesus who saves us. He has a really good grip on us and that is the most important factor—no power can "snatch" us out of His Hand.[1] However, we too need to exercise our grip on grace and here's why: Free will remains in play. God had to work *through* our free will to get us to accept His salvation. Just as He *wants* to save everyone, but can only save those who freely choose to let Him do it, so too He wants to *keep* everyone saved, but we have to freely choose to let Him do that as well.[2]

Consider the main New Testament description of our salvation, our "key" for understanding the basics:

For by grace you have been saved through faith, and that not of yourselves; it is the gift of God, not of works, that no one would boast. Ephesians 2:8-9 WEB

This powerful statement declares to us the unchanging basis of our salvation, binding together salvation, God's grace and ourselves. Even so, this golden chain of salvation has a "weak link" in it. First, let's examine the three unbreakable parts of the chain:

1. Salvation is God's idea and His passionate, unchanging desire for all of us. The Father chose us to be saved from before the worlds began. In His love for us He sent Jesus to the cross. Jesus fully

accomplished all that was necessary for us to be saved through His death and resurrection. *Nothing can change this.*

2. Grace is God's eternal nature. He is always full of compassion, love, understanding and mercy for us. By His mercy-filled heart He made a way to cover our sins through the atoning death of His Son. This is His unending gift of grace to every one of us. You cannot sin a sin that is not already forgiven by God and covered with the Blood of Jesus. *Nothing can change this.*

3. Saving faith is part of the free gift of salvation that He has prepared for us.[3] Faith doesn't save us— grace does. Grace is the Father's love. Grace is Jesus' sacrifice. Grace is the gift of the Spirit. When we seek Him to be saved, grace also provides a "gift of faith" in what Jesus has done. God gives this to us without "take backs"! You may not always have enough faith, trust and belief to resist sin or be confident about God's love for you, but you *always* have the gift of faith inside of you reminding you that Jesus is Savior and Lord. *Nothing can change this.*

The only thing that can possibly change is our will. Our freedom to choose is as real as it is deadly. We could choose life or death before we encountered Jesus and we can still choose life or death now that we know Him.[4] It was choosing to trust God as our Savior that got us saved in the first place. Consistently choosing against trusting our lives to God and His way of saving us, is where the possibility of losing salvation comes in.

By God's own decree the free gift cannot be forced upon anyone. He has given the power to choose life or death *to us*. No matter how desperately everyone needs His salvation, God does not force saving faith upon them. This is the enormity of the free will issue: Not all will be saved. Why? Because of their sins? Never! Jesus' death fully atoned for everyone's sins! Because God doesn't want them saved? Impossible! The Father doesn't want anyone to be lost![5]

The Crucial Role of Our Will

The heart-breaking tragedy is that people are going to hell every day whose sins are fully atoned for by Jesus and who are fully loved and desired by Father God.[6] *No one has to go to hell!* However, if we use our free will to reject the only One who can save us from the hell our sins deserve, where else is there for us to go? That's how powerful free will is in the hands of an unbeliever! The lost can so "No!" to God and make it stick from here to eternity.

This relationship between our freedom of will and God's grace-giving way of saving sinful humanity shows us the key to *staying* saved. First, let's use it in reverse: Can our sins "un-save" us? Never! Jesus' death has fully atoned for everyone's sins! Might God turn against us and "un-save" us? Impossible! The Father doesn't want anyone to be lost. If we can't lose our salvation due to our sins and if God is never going to turn against us, then what can possibly "un-save" us? *That little word "through"!*

We who are being saved have been given the gift of saving faith: We know who Jesus is (as Lord and Savior) and we know what He did for us. This is our opening to God. By the faith that came into us through the new birth, we are looking to Jesus, hoping in Him and trusting in Him to save us. We may be doing it very imperfectly, but even if our faith seems pathetically weak to us, God still sees that we want His salvation and are therefore giving Him permission to save us. Saving faith and all that the new birth make available to us cannot be taken from us. *Even the gift of faith cannot be changed!*

But we may *choose* not to let God's grace work *through* our faith to save us. If you are like me, you're saying "Never! I would never not want to be saved! I could never turn against God and Jesus like that!" I agree it seems impossible. But it is, nevertheless, a real danger. I believe that is why there are so many warnings in the New Testament, repeatedly calling us to persevere in faith and faithfulness.[7] Keep in mind that the New Testament warnings were primarily given to Christian believers. For more on this see the next chapter, "Can I Lose My Salvation?"

How could any believer turn against his own salvation? At the time of this writing I have been a Christian for thirty years and a priest for twenty. I have seen many believers fall into all kinds of terrible sins, yet turn from them and be restored by the almost unbelievable patience and grace of God. But I have also seen some be swallowed up by their sins, so that it has bent and twisted even their thinking and believing about God and Jesus.

I have also seen the terrible reality of people who have died in their sins—with their sins blazing red hot, so to speak—and with no apparent sign of repentance. This is a far cry from how most people live out their faith. It is remote, but it is real. Your faith may not seem to be working for you at times, but *whatever you do, don't stop working your faith!*

The Miracle Key

The key to staying saved is calling on the Name of the Lord. The promise God gives us is universal and absolute no matter what condition we are in: All who call on His Name *will be* saved.

> **For everyone who calls upon the name of the Lord** [invoking Him as Lord] **will be saved.**
> Romans 10:13 AMP

So whatever else you do, be sure to call and keep on calling on His Name. What's the rule? No minimum or maximum is indicated in the text, but my rule has always been: *Call as much as you need to, as often as you need to, for as long as you need to!* Even though the promised help doesn't always show up immediately with swords swinging, it always comes. Eventually, you will discover an increase of strength to resist the temptation. Eventually, you will find yourself moving through the trial towards the "other side." Eventually, you will once again be floating in the river of peace, basking under an open heaven. Never quit! Never give up! Saving help will always come... when you call and *keep* calling on His Mighty Name.

Prayers

Father, thank You that You always want to save me and will never reject me or forsake me. Thank You that saving me has been Your idea all along. You chose me to be saved before You created the worlds! Please keep forgiving my unbelief and working to increase my faith in the greatness of Your love for me and the steadfastness of Your promises to me.

Jesus, thank You for rescuing me by going to the cross and taking the punishment I deserved. You have covered all of my sins through Your death and resurrection. Please forgive me for those times when I'm afraid my sins aren't covered. As big as my sins are and as big as they sometimes feel, they are still nothing compared to Your sacrifice! Thank You for laying down Your life for me. Help me always to call on Your Name.

Holy Spirit, thank You that You have freely chosen to live within me. You are always working to keep my faith alive by reminding me to trust in the Father's love and to call on Jesus for help. You are with me even when I can't feel You. You are strengthening me even when I'm at my weakest. You are helping me hang on even when I feel like letting go. Never let me stop calling on the Name of the Lord!

---

[1] John 10:28: *I give them eternal life, and they will never perish, and no one will snatch them out of my hand.*

[2] These two scriptures have been given us by God to assure us that He wants everyone to be saved: 1 Timothy 2:3-4: *God our Savior, who desires all people to be saved and to come to the knowledge of the truth;* 2 Peter 3:9: *The Lord… is patient toward you, not wishing that any should perish, but that all should reach repentance.*

---

[3] Romans 5:1-2: *Through him we have also obtained access by faith into this grace in which we stand;* See also Romans 5:15-17, 6:23 for more on salvation as "free gift."

[4] We always have the power and the responsibility to choose between good and evil. Two things hinder us: We often don't truly know what is right or we aren't sufficiently motivated to do it. Even so, God does not excuse us from our moral duty: Deuteronomy 30:19-20 AMP: *I call heaven and earth to witness this day against you that I have set before you life and death, the blessings and the curses; therefore choose life, that you and your descendants may live. And may love the Lord your God, obey His voice, and cling to Him.*

[5] 1 Timothy 2:3-4; previously cited.

[6] Romans 3:22-25; previously cited, endnotes Chapter 7.

[7] These are just a sample of the many warning texts. I will include more in the next chapter: Colossians 1:21-23: *And you, who once were alienated and hostile in mind, doing evil deeds, he has now reconciled in his body of flesh by his death, in order to present you holy and blameless and above reproach before him, if indeed you <u>continue in the faith, stable and steadfast,</u> not shifting from the hope of the gospel that you heard;* Mark 13:13 AMP: *And you will be hated and detested by everybody for My name's sake, but he who patiently <u>perseveres and endures to the end</u> will be saved (made a partaker of the salvation by Christ, and delivered from spiritual death).*

CHAPTER 14

CAN I LOSE MY SALVATION?

This question has to be answered and answered well or we will have very little confidence during our times of stress and distress. We not only need confidence that we cannot lose the salvation and favor we are now receiving; we don't want that confidence based on a false hope. We certainly don't want to get down the road and wake up to disaster like the hapless virgins with no oil in their lamps that Jesus warned us about![1]

There is a long-standing controversy in church history over whether a Christian can lose the free gift of salvation. Eventually, you will need to decide what you are going to base your sense of security on so that you will be able to keep standing in confident faith when the enemy comes to accuse you of not really being saved. Don't think he won't! He does it at times with all of us. That's just the way it is.[2]

If you are a new believer, then you need to know up front that *Yes!* you can stay saved and be fully assured of your salvation every step of the way home to heaven. The God of All Grace who is saving you definitely is working with you to help you stay saved and to keep you in joyful confidence about it. This chapter will help you better understand staying saved.

If you are a seasoned believer, but still have little confidence of your salvation and are often plagued by fears of losing it, then you need to be reminded that you have an enemy who is aptly named the "Accuser of the Brethren," who has no power to separate you from

God, but who desperately strives to rob you of your peace and confidence in God as your Savior.[3] This chapter will help you understand what is required of you for staying saved, but you may need to revisit how you can know with assurance that you are saved.

All of us who believe would love to enjoy in every moment the "blessed assurance" that we are saved, are staying saved and will make it home to heaven. And we can! Even in our worst moments of weakness and temptation we can be wonderfully confident that our salvation is not in jeopardy. We can "reach through to heaven" by faith and access the full joy of our salvation at any time, since it is not based on our circumstances but on God's gift. "All it takes" is learning to believe God's truth instead of your feelings.[4]

A Difference of Opinion

There are two schools of thought on this matter of security, two sometimes warring camps in the Body of Christ. Some believe that it is impossible for a Christian to lose the free gift of salvation.[5] This straightforward position is called "the perseverance of the saints", "eternal security" or "once saved, always saved." Others believe that salvation is indeed a free gift of grace received through faith in Christ, but that a Christian must persevere in their relationship with Christ to maintain their salvation.[6] It is possible to lose one's salvation, but genuine security is also possible. This paradoxical position is called "conditional security."

One reason for the division is that scripture (as you will often discover) can be interpreted in various ways.

The problem is not with God or the Bible, but with us. We are the ones being drawn "out of darkness into His marvelous light."[7] It is easy for us to get things wrong due to either our lack of knowledge and experience or our "itching ears"—the desire to hear what we *wish* was true.[8]

This is a very important issue! Nothing less than our eternal destination is at stake, so of course there are strong feelings and careful reasoning on either side of the divide. Let's look at the pros and cons of both positions:

1. Position 1: Salvation cannot be lost; security is absolute. Obviously, if you choose to believe this there is an opportunity to have a powerful sense of security and confidence about your own salvation and the salvation of your loved ones. There are a lot of scriptures to back up this position, so it is fairly easily defensible against any condemning or accusing attack of the enemy. I believed it myself for the first fifteen years of my life in Christ and it really helped me to maintain a confidence in God and keep my "helmet of salvation" firmly planted on my head.[9] These are the pros.

The cons are that there are simply too many serious warnings in the New Testament given to believers that their salvation can be lost.[10] This is the problem coming from scripture and it is the one that eventually made me shift to the second position. The other main problem is that Jesus stated the principle that wisdom is proved by her children and that a tree is known by its fruit.[11] The sad observation is that many people, who embrace some form of

85

eternal security as their covering—regardless of their denomination—seem to behave as if living for the Lord doesn't matter! It seems to be "telling" people who believe it that now that you're saved, you're home free no matter what. Such complacency creates a dangerous sense of security. Instead of "waking up," resisting the enemy and seeking the Lord, believers are lulled into the sleep of sin instead.

A further problem with this position is the explanation given for why believers fall into sin. It is maintained that the person who has had a genuine conversion is guaranteed to persevere in the faith, because God will see to it that they do. The emphasis is on God's sovereignty with little allowance for the operation of free will: If God chose you, then you *will* be saved and you *will* persevere! Therefore, when people who think they are Christians fall into grievous sin, they could not have been genuine believers to begin with. Their experience of belief in Christ, no matter how real it seems to them, must be due to a "false conversion." This can open the door to endless introspection: "Was I sincere enough? Were my motives pure enough? Did I really confess *all* my sins? Am I saved?" Such subjectivism is a trap which bears absolutely no resemblance to Paul's clear description of saving faith in Romans 10:9.

2. Position 2: Salvation can be lost, but security is real. You have to learn how to embrace both paradox and mystery to live with this one (our God is like that at times), but the sense of security it provides is at least equal to anything "eternal security" offers and it has none of the unpleasant side effects noted above.

The "danger" with this position is not so much being complacent about sin, but failing to receive the true sense of security it offers. Realizing the need to stay connected to the Lord, keeps us resisting the enemy and fighting against sin—with perseverance, not necessarily perfection. However, this lack of perfection in the struggle can easily lead to anxiety and insecurity, unless we have a strong grip on grace. That "strong grip" is exactly what needs to be cultivated!

Staying Saved Is a Faith Issue

For this second position to work we first have to clear out of the way a huge problem or there will never be any sense of security coming to us. Do *not* make the mistake of trying to judge if you are saved by your "works" or by your "fruit." Believe me; you will never have enough of either to satisfy the devil's accusations! The Accuser will hammer you in your conscience over any infraction, lapse or failure doing his best to make it seem you aren't saved and won't be saved. However, the truth is that we are saved by grace through faith, *not by our works*! Since we cannot get saved by our works, we cannot get "unsaved" *by our works* (or lack of them).

For by grace you have been saved through faith, and that not of yourselves; it is the gift of God, not of works, that no one would boast. Ephesians 2:8-9 WEB

The key factor is the phrase "through faith." Our salvation is a faith issue, not a works issue! This is not the way it seems that it should be, nor is it the way it *feels* that it is (especially when we've goofed up), but according to scripture it *is* the way that it is. Since I am saved by grace through believing in Jesus, I can only become "unsaved" *through not believing*. This renouncing of the faith surely seems impossible to any new believer. How could anyone turn against Jesus? How could anyone turn against the faith in Him that brings so great a salvation? I have spoken to this in "How Can I Stay Saved?", so for now let's press on to the final answer to the question we started with: Can I lose my salvation?

Yes. It can be lost. You can chose (in some way) to repudiate your faith in Jesus.[12] You can reject your own salvation. Admittedly, that is scary. Again I have to say, how could anyone who has been shown Jesus and the gospel be crazy enough to reject Him? Yet, consider this: If you have freedom of will to choose to be saved; you also have freedom of will to reject salvation. You do not have *less* freedom of will after meeting Jesus, you actually have *more*. People can and do turn against their original faith in Jesus due to hurtful life experiences, defective discipleship, or by clinging to known sin, rather than determinedly calling on Christ to deliver them. The dangerous reality of having a free will, however, is obviously not where the powerful and genuine security comes from.

The Blessed Assurance

The security that upholds me every moment of every day (now that I have settled into believing it) is based on a faith-knowing of these five factors:

1) My salvation *cannot* be based on me in any way. I am convinced that in me dwells no good thing apart from Jesus.[13] I can do nothing without Him.[14] He knows it. I know it. God is not looking to me to deserve His salvation. That would be impossible for me and it would make grace of no value. The grace of salvation is *always* a gift and it is *always* being extended to (though not forced upon) me.[15]

2) God *always* wants to save me. His love for me is perfect. Nothing can change this or take it from me.

3) The Blood of Jesus covers *every* sin I could possibly sin. Nothing can change this or take it from me.[16]

4) I have already received saving faith if I know who Jesus is as Savior and Lord, for if you can confess He is Lord and believe God raised Him from the dead (as Savior from sin), then you have saving faith. Nothing can take this from me.[17]

5) So long as I cling to believing the truth about who Jesus is and I persevere in calling on His Name, then my salvation is secure for the promise is clearly written that *all* who call on His Name shall be

saved.[18] Yes, I will likely have frequent bouts of intense struggle with sin, but of course I am going to call on His Name! And so are you! *How hard is that?*

Just make sure that you don't allow yourself to start turning against God and Jesus and the salvation that they offer. They won't turn against you (all sins have been atoned for) or turn off the grace they send your way. As long as you want it, it is yours. *But it will not be forced on anyone.* So, don't ever let sin begin to make you want to shut yourself off from the very One whose salvation you need!

Prayer

Father it is scary to think I could lose this salvation. Keep my focused on living for You and calling on Your Name. Thank You that Your love perfectly covers me, the Blood of Jesus fully atones for my sins, and You have given the Holy Spirit to live within me. I know I don't have to be perfect, but help me to persevere in seeking to be faithful!

---

[1] In Matthew 25:1-13 Jesus tells the story of the foolish virgins who were unprepared to meet the bridegroom when he returned. That they had no oil for their lamps is a telling sign that the holy fire of a living faith had gone out, yet they had done nothing to remedy the situation.

[2] 1 Peter 5:8-9: *Be sober-minded; be watchful. Your adversary the devil prowls around like a roaring lion, seeking someone to devour.*

[3] Revelation 12:10 KJV: *For the accuser of our brethren is cast down, which accused them before our God day and night.*

[4] I put "all it takes" in quotes because although believing God's truth over our feelings is certainly doable, it can be extremely difficult.

5 Called Calvinism after John Calvin the French Reformed theologian (1509-1564). He taught that grace cannot be resisted; that God saves everyone He wills to save; and that those who have experienced true conversion will persevere faithfully to the end. Not our position.

6 Called Arminianism after the Dutch Reformed theologian Jacobus Arminius (1560-1609). He held that grace could be resisted and that believers are not beyond the possibility of falling from grace (ie. God cannot save everyone due to their free will; even the "saved" can reject the faith they have received). This is the position taken here.

7 1 Peter 2:9: *Him who called you out of darkness into his marvelous light.*

8 2 Timothy 4:3-4: *Having itching ears they will accumulate for themselves teachers to suit their own passions.*

9 1 Thessalonians 5:8: *...and for a helmet the hope of salvation.*

10 Here are a few outstanding examples of New Testament warning texts directed to followers of Jesus: Matthew 10:28, 25:1-13; Luke 12:5; Romans 1:28-32; 1 Corinthians 5:3-5, 6:9-13; Ephesians 5:3-12; Colossians 3:5-11; 1 Timothy 6:11-13; Hebrews 2:1-4, 4:11-13, 5:11-6:12, 10:26-39, 12:25-29; Revelation 2: 19-24, 3:1-6, 21:7-8. Why give so many deadly serious warnings, unless there is a) real danger ahead and b) something we can do to avoid it?

11 Matthew 11:19 AMP: *Yet wisdom is justified and vindicated by what she does (her deeds) and by her children;* Matthew 12:33: *Either make the tree good and its fruit good... for the tree is known by its fruit.*

12 Jesus' brother Jude warned against departing the faith. Those who follow ungodly passions and sensuality "deny our only Master": Jude 4: *For certain people have crept... who pervert the grace of our God into sensuality and deny our only Master and Lord, Jesus Christ.*

13 Paul puts our moral bankruptcy bluntly: Romans 7:18-19: *For I know that nothing good dwells in me, that is, in my flesh. For I have the desire to do what is right, but not the ability to carry it out.*

14 Never one to flatter us, Jesus says it plainly: John 15:5: *Apart from me you can do nothing.*

15 God is always for us: Romans 8:33-35, 39 WEB: *Who could bring a charge against God's chosen ones? It is God who justifies. Who is he who condemns? It is Christ who died... [Nothing] will be able to separate us from the love of God, which is in Christ Jesus our Lord.* See also 1 John 4:18.

16 Every sin we may ever sin was atoned for before we were born: Ephesians 1:6-7 WEB: *In whom we have our redemption through his blood, the forgiveness of our trespasses, according to the riches of his grace.*

17 Romans 10:9; previously cited, p 72.

18 Romans 10:13; previously cited, p 73.

CHAPTER 15

HOW CAN I STOP SINNING?

You are a "sin terminator!" You are death to sin and a danger to the enemy and his cohorts. That's part of your new assignment and new capabilities. You are now reborn as a lover of God. That makes you automatically an enemy of God's enemies—Satan and his kingdom of darkness which work through sin. Until now you have been a "slave to sin." You could not help but live separated from God due to the original sin of Adam which had you blinded and bound.[1] Before Christ appeared you were centered on Self; now you are free to live centered on Christ. And because you *know* God through your faith in Christ, you can now live *for Him*, rather than yourself. That's the game changer.

This radical change of allegiance means that you will inevitably want to see your life from God's perspective, especially when it comes to the right and wrong of things. His perspective on sin is so very different from ours! We coddle it; He wants it crushed. We excuse it; He rebukes it. We make room for it; He works to crowd it out. Always remember that God *loves* you; it is sin that He hates. You are not your sins. No one is, not unless they (God forbid) die in their sins with no repentance. You, however, have asked God to forgive you and save you from your sins. This He has done by justifying you. Now begins the lifelong process of separating you from your sins as the Word and the Holy Spirit lead the way. The goal is for you to separate from sin before it separates you from God. All sins separate us from God, but not to the same degree.

1. Deal Breakers. These are obvious and outward sins. They are the worst. Most of them can be classified as "sins of the flesh" since they either come through physical desires or they are expressed through us in obvious, outward ways that directly impact others. These have to be stoutly resisted and eliminated *and they can be!* They are completely unacceptable for Christians and are actually unbearable to experience *as* a Christian, because conscience—quickened by the Holy Spirit—really "kills" you over these!

Paul lists them at several different places in scripture.[2] Always these sins are condemned in the strongest possible terms. Continuing in them without repentance (without seeking continually to get free, crying out to God and struggling faithfully until God's deliverance arrives) *guarantees* a miserable life on earth. It also raises the very real possibility of an eternity united to that sin and its punishment, rather than being united to the Lord. Choosing sin is always in some degree a rejection of Jesus and God. That's why these more deadly sins carry such stringent warnings.

2. Joy Slayers. All the way on the other side of the scale are "soul sins," such as pride, fear, worry, unforgiveness, etc. These are often hidden and inward. These also separate from God, but they are not (thankfully) as dangerous to one's salvation. It often takes a while before we become aware of them as sins, since they seem like such "natural" emotional reactions. It's just the way we are, or so we say. The truth is quite different: Anything that doesn't look or sound like Jesus in you, isn't the real you! That would be the *old* you, the former version of yourself that now needs to be put to death so that Christ in you can arise.[3]

The Battle for Your Freedom

Everyone is pestered by these "smaller" sins to differing degrees, depending upon personal history.[4] With practice they can be identified by their fruit: It is impossible to entertain a sinful thought or heart attitude and enjoy the peace of Christ at the same time. However, since we are often oblivious to them as sins, we truly are dependent upon others in the Body of Christ noticing them, so that they can pray to the Lord for our deliverance or speak to us in a loving and concerned way that might turn the lights on for us.[5]

No matter what the sin is (major, minor, or anything in between) the process of getting free and the power for gaining victory are the same for all.[6] The unvarying rule is: Whenever you recognize a sin in you, you are obligated to separate from it. Don't take on guilt over being tempted. You can't stop the urge or the allure from showing up, though with time the Lord will cause both its power and its reappearances to diminish. But you *always* have it within your power to say "No!" to the temptation and not let it get your allegiance.

You are a free person only as long as you don't allow sin to "reign" in you.[7] Your freedom is worth fighting for! Jesus bled and died to give you the chance to live as a free person united to God, not just to rescue you from hell. He paid sin's penalty so He could free you from its power.

You will need to grow two things to help you defeat sin's power over you. Studying the scriptures will help to grow these two things, but mere knowledge of the scriptures is insufficient to stop you from sinning. For that you will need a genuine knowledge of God. This comes in two forms:

1. A Great Love of God and Jesus. To know Jesus is to love Him. To truly know the Father is to happily yield one's whole life in perfect trust to the One who loves you best. To know the Holy Spirit intimately is to confidently enjoy His power and presence in every aspect of daily life. Not there yet? None of us "have arrived." However, if you have now been graced with knowing Jesus, you are off to a good start. The tender side of the love of God carries warm to blazing affections; the "tough-as-nails" side is sustained by cultivating a fierce loyalty to the One who set you free by his agonizing death on the cross.

2. A Healthy Fear of God. One element of this is respect for the reality of consequences ruled over by God. No one gets away with anything! We always reap what we sow, whether we sow to the flesh by sinning or sow to the spirit by trusting and obeying the Lord.[8] Sow so that you can reap, not weep! But do not allow yourself to take on any fear that God may be mad at you (He never is), or that He doesn't want to save you (He always does) or that He is condemning you for your sinfulness (He never condemns, nor does He accuse).

You can and should work to remove specific sins, but you cannot remove sinfulness itself. Your old nature is a cesspool of bad attitudes and wrong ideas and it will continue to bubble up evil throughout your days. But you don't have to walk in it! As we trust Jesus, the Holy Spirit helps us walk in His better ways. In turning to face the light of Christ by looking to Jesus and walking with Him, our old nature is laid to rest behind us like a shadow. However, returning to walk in the ways of the Shadow (putting Self first) makes the old nature grow stronger and longer.

More Motivations

The essential elements for staying connected to the Lord include continual prayer, daily Bible reading, weekly worship, heart-to-heart fellowship with other believers and finding a Spirit directed outlet for service. Stay steady in all five and the Lord will use them like "safety nets" to keep you well connected to Him, giving you victories in your struggles and providing opportunities for Him to catch you, if you start to fall away. Jesus actively pursued doing these five things during His days on earth and He still loves doing them: Learn to do them with Him, through Him and for Him.

You have to have reasons for staying faithful that are bigger than your own comfort and pleasures. There is a sea of hurting, lost humanity all around you that truly needs you to put sin to death and walk with the Lord so that He can reach some of them through you. Your family and friends also need you to walk closely with the Lord, whether they realize it or not. Your life will inevitably impact them for better or worse. Let that knowledge work for you. These are powerful motivations.

Become passionate about finding out what God has for you. It is something really good, but you will only find out if you trust Him enough to fight your sins to death so that He can raise you into His life. You have a purpose and a destiny to discover and pursue. These cannot arrive in your life without your full cooperation. Sin will obstruct the path to your God-envisioned future or work to derail it if you do find it. Don't let your guard down!

Well aright! I don't want to dwell too much on the enemy and his works. We are primarily lovers of God and liberators of others. To be that, we have to be ready to "fight the good fight" of faith whenever those moments of wrestling with the tempter appear. Thankfully, the walk is primarily a stroll in the park beside our awesome God and Friend.[9] We fight off the enemy so that we can keep enjoying our new-found freedom to live in intimate union with Christ.[10] The goal of this primer has been to help you become saved through faith in Jesus Christ and then to give you a heads-up for how to live the Christian life you have now begun. You will need much more than this whenever the real trials arrive. In the meantime, here is the secret to successful Christian living: The new life is meant to be lived on the same graced basis by which it has begun. Indeed, it can be lived in no other way...

Prayer

Father, strengthen me for the days ahead! Help me cultivate a great heart of love for You, so that I will call on Your Name and seek You out in my times of temptation or trial. And grant that I would also grow that healthy "fear of God" which will keep me fighting to stay on the path when love alone doesn't seem like enough to hold me to it.

Jesus, please come and grow in me those same things that You loved to do when You walked the earth. Help me plunge into the Bible as into refreshing streams of heavenly truth. Teach to pray and assist me in discovering all of the ways of communication with God that You also enjoyed. Lead me through the veil into times of glorious worship. Bring into my own life the kind of fellowship with others that You enjoyed with Your "band of brothers." Finally, grow my own heart in Your way of loving service to others.

Holy Spirit, please come! I will need You reminding me, coaching me, encouraging me, teaching me and (no doubt) correcting me. I cannot do this without You. Help me learn to entrust myself to Your abiding presence and to Your power poured out on my behalf. Draw me into every aspect of the new life that God has set before me. Spur me on to run into that destined future where all of my gifts and passions get released in glad-hearted service for my God.

---

[1] Jesus has come to free us from sinning, not just from being punished for sinning! John 8:34-36: *Everyone who commits sin is a slave to sin... So if the Son sets you free, you will be free indeed.*

[2] See 1 Corinthians 5:9-13, Ephesians 5:3-12 and 3:5-11. Sins common to these lists include idolatry, sexual sin, homosexuality, covetousness (greed), reviling, drunkenness (and by extension all substance abuse).

[33] This former side of ourselves is variously described as "the flesh", the "fallen nature", the "old man", the "carnal self" or "sinful nature": Romans 8:13 AMP: *For if you live according to [the dictates of] the flesh, you will surely die…*

[4] I use "minor" with this caution: When the Lord puts His finger on a sin He wants us to forsake, it never seems very minor at the time!

[5] Ephesians 4:15-16: *Rather, speaking the truth in love, we are to grow up in every way into him who is the head, into Christ.*

[6] Our website, Healingstreamsusa.org, is dedicated to helping people get free of these emotional/spiritual sins. All such negative emotional stress robs many Christians of their rightful peace, joy and freedom of spirit. Don't let that be you! Explore what we offer.

[7] The following passage is from the Amplified Bible which is a great translation to have on hand for study purposes: Romans 6:12-13 AMP: *Let not sin therefore rule as king in your mortal (short-lived, perishable) bodies, to make you yield to its cravings and be subject to its lusts and evil passions…*

[8] Galatians 6:8: *For the one who sows to his own flesh will from the flesh reap corruption, but the one who sows to the Spirit will from the Spirit reap eternal life.*

[9] 1 Timothy 6:12: *Fight the good fight of the faith. Take hold of the eternal life.*

[10] Galatians 2:20; previously cited, endnotes Chapter 7.

CHAPTER 16

HOW DO I LIVE NOW THAT I AM SAVED?

This is the best part! We get to live by the same graceful means by which we got saved in the first place. We pray and trust, pray and trust, trust and follow, trust and follow. It is meant to be "child's play" with some embattled times in between. Don't settle for a walk with the Lord that is only embattled! And don't go back to serving the unholy trinity of Satan, sin and Self. All along we were created to live for Jesus by listening to Him and obeying Him.

Trust is the key to victories. Trust keeps us well connected to the Lord. Trust is how we position our heart so that the Holy Spirit can lift us and lead us into the flow of the new life. It all goes along "swimmingly" so long as we keep trusting. Yes, that is the hard part. Jesus knows this. That is why He described believing in God as the "work" that we are meant to do.[1]

You may be thinking, "But it is soooo hard for me to trust. I don't trust anyone—not even myself! Everyone has let me down!" This is actually an advantage. If you know that there is nowhere else to put your trust, then you are ready to start putting it in the one place where it should have been placed all along—in God!

"But He is invisible! How can I trust someone I can't see?" This is why He has given His Word to us. We can see His Word and hold His Word in our hands. We have His promises, His truths and His guarantees in writing! He has staked His reputation as a truthful, dependable God on His Word being true and His promises being dependable.[2]

Even Jesus Had to "Work" at Trusting

Jesus, facing His worst moments in the Garden, cried out to His Father, "Your Word is Truth!"[3] Jesus "bet His life" on God's Word being true. We follow His lead and bet our lives again and again on things in God's Word that the Holy Spirit is teaching us to believe. Then as we trust ourselves to God, God demonstrates to us how trust-worthy He really is. But you have to trust Him to find that out! Here is how Paul described the high flying life of trust-filled love:

> **I have been crucified with Christ** [in Him I have shared His crucifixion]; **it is no longer I who live, but Christ (the Messiah) lives in me; and the life I now live in the body I live by faith in (by adherence to and reliance on and complete trust in) the Son of God, Who loved me and gave Himself up for me.** Galatians 2:20 AMP

The main thing to grasp is that you live the new life in exactly the same way that you entered the new life: by grace through faith.[4] Just as you trusted Jesus to be God's way of getting you to heaven, you also trust Jesus to be God's way of getting a heavenly life to you down here. You are saved—brought into true life—by grace through faith every step of the way![5]

You had no way of solving the "what-do-I-do-about-death" problem, did you? But you are not worried about it now because you can see that Jesus will help you when the time comes. In the same way, you are certainly going to encounter all kinds of problems in life that you can't see how to solve. Only some of these will be sin problems. Many of them will just be the garden variety problems of daily life. Jesus is your all purpose Savior, Helper and Guide for life. Looking to Jesus, trusting Him and following Him will allow God to lead you into a new way of living (without so much stress, anxiety and despair) and new results.

Prayer

Father, You know that there are plenty of times when trust doesn't come easily to me. Yet, now I see that trust is the key to living the new life of grace. May You, Jesus and the Holy Spirit work with me and raise me to this "higher" way of living. I don't know the way to get there, but You do! Lead into the bright Spirit-filled freedom of my new life in Christ!

---

[1] John 6:28-30: *This is the work of God, that you believe in him whom he has sent.*

[2] Hebrews 6:17-19: *So when God desired to show more convincingly to the heirs of the promise the unchangeable character of his purpose, he guaranteed it with an oath…*

[3] "Sanctification" describes the work of God in cleansing us from lies and false beliefs and the sins they engender: John 17:17 AMP: *Sanctify them [purify, consecrate, separate them for Yourself, make them holy] by the Truth; Your Word is Truth.*

[4] Colossians 2:6-7: *Therefore, as you received Christ Jesus the Lord, so walk in him, rooted and built up in him and established in the faith…*

[5] Ephesians 2:8-9; previously cited, endnotes for Chapter 2.

CHAPTER 17

WHAT ARE MY FIRST STEPS?

No one needs to tell the brand new Christian what their first steps should be. These will flow with the natural grace of a stream surging forth when it is undammed. The heart freshly filled with realizations of liberation by sins forgiven, by God's love revealed and by the way to heaven opening wide cannot help but ascend upwards with prayers, praise and thanksgiving. Ordinary events, the world of people and all of nature may be seen in a whole new light, under the glow of divinely kindled new passions.

The flow of these spiritually assisted feelings may likely lead the new believer into finding a church, reading the Bible and sharing about Jesus with their friends. All of this is very good! Yet even here it will be helpful to see that this is not just you (if you are that new believer), but it is Jesus *in* you. He is your new life!

Jesus loves doing these things and will always seek to help you do them, even when you don't want to. By the Holy Spirit Jesus is now inside of you awakening and assisting all of these new, right and delightful desires. Your old feelings may return to "drown out" the new ones, but the truth is that the real you is now joined to Jesus and wants what He wants and desires what He desires. You must, however, prepare for the absence of this "starter kit" of good feelings.

It is commonly observed that conversion experiences often usher in what's called a "honeymoon" period where God makes it easy for the new believer to trust in

Him and rejoice in loving Jesus. The Lord pours out "extra grace" so that our spirits can soar assisted by His Spirit. If this is your experience please realize that it will not last! By all means enjoy it, but take good advantage of the new sense of empowerment that it gives you to anchor your life in Christ with the necessary "tools" of a long "marriage" to your Bridal Lover. Honeymoons are something anyone can enjoy: Successful, happily fulfilled marriages require a lot of work!

You have an enemy in the dark one and his vassals (evil spirits) who will stop at nothing to bring you down once the initial grace begins to wear off. Jesus warned that the seed which is planted can easily be uprooted by the enemy.[1] Therefore, some of your first steps should be ones that will prepare you for the challenges and trials which Jesus says will surely come on account of the truths you have received.

"Tools" for Your New Life in Christ

Jesus is the "key" to everything! He is the Main Event and the Greatest Person in your world and this universe. Now that you know it, your primary concern is going to be to stick close to Him, since He is the source of all the good things flowing into your life and He is the One your heart most deeply and powerfully loves and cannot live without. He is far more than your gateway to heaven; He *is* Life.[2]

If you drift away from walking closely with Him, you will naturally begin to lose life's best qualities. It is impossible to find a full and complete life apart from Him, because He is both *life* itself and the *way* to live life.[3] He is also your *truth*.[4] You are seeing so many things right now by the light of Christ, but if you drift away from His perspective on your life and this world, you cannot help but drift into darkness and oppression.[5] Don't let that happen!

Consider these tried and proven ways of staying close to Jesus:

1. Follow His Example. Get to know Jesus through the gospels and then try to let His way of handling things become yours.

2. Live within His Boundaries. Jesus sets the moral boundaries. Anything outside them guarantees an unhappy life! Everything you will ever truly need has already been placed on your path *within the moral boundaries*. Let Him teach you where the lines are drawn and don't let the enemy trick you into trespassing. The boundary lines are drawn in "pleasant places" to ensure that your life thrives.[6] You have His Word on that.

3. See through His Eyes. Scripture will help you learn to see everything in your life and in this world from Jesus' perspective. His Word is truth, the whole truth and nothing but the truth.[7] His perspective is the only one that counts! Whenever you are stuck in seeing things your way or the world's way, you will lose peace and fill up quickly with all kinds of unwanted emotions. However, anytime you regain His perspective you will regain your freedom and joy. Learn to really love truth.[8] Let scripture become your most trusted Friend.

4. Let Him Guide You. Jesus will seek to lead you within the wide boundaries of the moral law into doing all kinds of things that will expand your life, enhance your love for Him and help you discover your destined purposes for being here. The goal is to become a heaven-directed lover of God and liberator of people. So learn to listen for His voice, watch for His hand upon events, and especially become fine-tuned to the movements of His Spirit within you. There is a *lot* to learn in all these areas, but you are now a disciple, a "learner for life."[9]

5. Love and Trust; Trust and Obey. There is no other way to be happy in Jesus than to learn how to trust Him with everything going on in our lives and those of our loved ones and choosing to follow all that He asks of us. Since "we love Him, because He first loved us," whenever you find your feet slipping off the right path, run quickly back to Him, receive His mercy and recover your heart for your great Savior and Friend.[10] This makes it much easier to want to keep following Him.

There Is So Much More!

Love is all around you. Jesus is in you.[11] Grace is endless and very real. But so are challenges to growth. Fortunately, the Holy Spirit will watch over you and work to keep your challenges from being too overwhelming.[12] Let Him lead you step by step; stay in step with His leadings; and you will find your way through to freedom and a flow of peace that beggars description.

You may discover that you have issues from the past that just won't go away. The enemy doesn't play fair: he is certain to attack you where your emotions are most raw and vulnerable. The need for emotional or "inner" healing is real: We have a whole website devoted to it. Healingstreamsusa.org is a great place to go for recovering from emotional pain or traumas of the past. The 24 main healing lessons are available for free as mp3, mp4 and PDF downloads. Additional resources are listed at the back of this book. These will also help you learn to master your emotional state so that you will spend more time living in the deep, dreamy peace of Christ than you ever imagined possible, even under the duress and pressures of an active life.

Be sure that you seek out and find a church home.[13] Our God is the Father of an enormous family of redeemed children, extending all the way into heaven. In a loving, Bible-believing congregation you will strengthen your prayer life, gain understanding of scripture, enjoy opportunities for fellowship with other like-minded believers, encounter the Lord during times of anointed worship and discover your gifts and passion for service to others. I cannot stress this enough: These are the "Big Five" connecters that cultivate our new life in Christ, which Jesus *in us* loves to be doing.[14] We get to do them with Him! They are also divinely given "safety nets" which help hold us in place when we are under times of attack or temptation. Keep them in good repair—your life in Christ depends upon it. If you don't do these "do's" you are certain to end up doing the "don'ts"!

We are almost there now, at the starting point of your new beginning. What will your life in Christ be like? You are the one who gets to decide! To the degree that you commit and yield your life to Him, to that extent you will ultimately get to know Him. Jesus can only fully reveal Himself to those who trust Him enough to let Him lead them step by step into life as He has planned it.[15] So don't hold anything back! Give Jesus all you've got and you will never regret it. Press in to know your Savior *as your Lord* and in the bargain discover who you have been created to become.

Prayers

Father, it is exciting and a bit scary to be setting out on this journey. Thank You for all that you have done to save me and give me new life through faith in Your Son. I ask that You help me to love Jesus my Savior with my whole heart.

Jesus, You have given me so much! I owe my life and my hope of heaven to Your sacrifice. I give myself to You, holding nothing back. Let's head out on this adventure together!

Holy Spirit, lead me into all of the truths that will set me free to live in that glorious liberty of the children of God as You teach me how to deny myself and live for Jesus my Lord.

---

[1] See Mark 4:3-20; Luke 48:4-15 for the parable of the seed that fell on four different kinds of soil.

[2] John 1:3-4: *In him was life, and the life was the light of men.*

[3] John 14:6: *I am the way, and the truth, and the life.*

[4] John 1:14: *And the Word became flesh and dwelt among us.*

---

[5] 1 Peter 5:8-9: *Be sober-minded; be watchful. Your adversary the devil prowls around like a roaring lion, seeking someone to devour.*

[6] Psalm 16:6: *The lines have fallen for me in pleasant places; indeed, I have a beautiful inheritance.*

[7] John 17:17; previously cited, endnotes for Chapter 16.

[8] 2 Thessalonians 2:10 AMP: *And by unlimited seduction to evil and with all wicked deception for those who are perishing (going to perdition) because they did not welcome the Truth but refused to love it that they might be saved;* 2 Thessalonians 2:13: *God chose you as the firstfruits to be saved, through sanctification by the Spirit and belief in the truth.*

[9] The first disciples were twelve men who followed Jesus and were taught by Him as they walked along together. They still walk with Him.

[10] 1 John 4:19 WEB: *We love Him, because he first loved us.*

[11] Colossians 1:27: *This mystery, which is Christ in you, the hope of glory.*

[12] 1 Corinthians 10:13: *No temptation has overtaken you that is not common to man. God is faithful, and he will not let you be tempted beyond your ability, but with the temptation he will also provide the way of escape, that you may be able to endure it.*

[13] Hebrews 10:25 AMP: *Not forsaking or neglecting to assemble together [as believers], as is the habit of some people.*

[14] The "Big Five" are Bible, prayer, worship, fellowship and service (*Big Pigs Wear Fancy Shoes* if you need a way to remember them).

[15] Jeremiah 29:11: *For I know the plans I have for you, declares the Lord, plans for wholeness and not for evil, to give you a future and a hope.*

A FOND FAREWELL

I hope by now you have a growing confidence that you have done the right thing in looking to Jesus for your salvation. He is God's perfect answer to all of your salvation questions! It is so typical of life, however, that one answer leads into many more questions and one problem solved ushers in a fresh array of challenges. At least by now you have a good understanding of what the basics are. Really mastering them will take a lifetime of practical experience.

At the time of this writing I have entered my thirtieth year of walking with Jesus and still, I find myself daily re-discovering the all encompassing reality of what it means to be saved by grace. My need for Him seems endless! Good thing for me that His supply of mercy and saving help surpasses my need. Still, one of the most baffling mysteries of all is why trusting myself to Him *in everything* remains such a challenge.

I note this not to discourage you, my friend, but to relieve you at the outset (if it were possible) of the impossible burden of thinking you must achieve some kind of perfection with your faith. *Do the best you can and never quit!* There. That sums it up nicely. Have a great adventure in the Lord and tell me about it whenever the Lord weaves our lives together again, whether in this life or the next. Until then...

The Lord bless you and keep you, the Lord make His face shine upon you and be gracious unto you; the Lord lift up His countenance upon you and give you peace.

Bonus Section

To make ready for the Lord a people prepared.
Luke 1:17

THE STARTER KIT

If you are a new Christian, you need to know that even though you have been given a great starter kit of heavenly blessings, it carries no guarantee you will have a happy or wholesome life. Make sure you know what's in it, but don't stop there: Put it to good use gaining these three essential extras.

Everyone Gets Started with This

Our loving Father showered us with so much in the first moment of conversion that it takes a separate article just to list the things God was doing behind the scenes. One tragedy you will certainly want to avoid is having so many gifts, but not having the slightest idea what they are or how to access them. Not every Christian is aware of what God gave them in conversion. If you want to make sure that you are "in the know", review Chapter 7: "What Is the New Birth?

Practically every Christian is aware of what we are calling here, the starter kit. These are the obvious items of the new life that everyone seems to get. Other items may be like an inheritance in the bank from a distant relative—on deposit in our name, but possibly unknown to us. These items of the starter kit are in our spiritual hands for ready use from day one.

1) Knowing who Jesus is.
2) Experiencing the forgiveness of our sins.
3) Receiving the hope of heaven.

4) Having the Holy Spirit within us.

5) Believing that the Bible is God's Word.

That's a lot of spiritual capital! Check to make sure you have received these very important items in your starter kit. There are certainly other things that you may be aware of that you personally experienced or were shown in the moment of your conversion. Hold on to them too.

Nevertheless, as great as these five main elements of the starter kit are, you need to know that every other Christian was given them, but not every Christian lives a happy or wholesome life. Evidently, the starter kit it not enough to guarantee a desirable life for everyone. You will have to learn to press in to gain your full inheritance.[1]

Moving Beyond the Starter Kit

The following are three highly important aspects of the new life that you will have to intentionally go after, because they won't just come to you.

1) The Keys of the Kingdom. One major thing that goes beyond being born again is what Jesus said He would be giving to the disciples at Caesarea Philippi, the "keys to the Kingdom." Be sure to look these up.[2] Not knowing what they are or how to use them is a major reason why so many Christians never get healed of their past hurts and live defeated and broken lives in the present. The keys give us access to the joy, peace and right ways of living, as

well as the presence and power of the Holy Spirit. Don't leave home without them!

2) The Baptism of Power. Jesus also didn't want those early disciples to leave Jerusalem without something else: the baptism in the Holy Spirit.[3] This is often called the "second blessing" because it usually is not given in the moment of conversion, but has to be sought after and received later in the Christian's life

It was given to the first disciples a full 50 days after they received the indwelling Holy Spirit directly from the Risen Christ. After Jesus' ascension they huddled in the upper room in prayer seeking this empowerment, not really knowing what it would be like or when it might come. Then on the great Day of Pentecost the Spirit came down upon them all and raised the previously born-again disciples to a new level of spiritual empowerment.

3) Trust and Obedience. You will definitely need a holy and rugged determination to keep your focus on Jesus by seeking to trust and follow Him with every step you take. An old gospel hymn expresses this truth perfectly: "There is no other way to be happy in Jesus, but to trust and obey."[4]

Being faithful doesn't mean being perfect. True moral perfection is not possible for any of us, even with the full help of heaven. Faithfulness means you are doing your level best to live in a way that would be pleasing to the Lord. This means believing in Him enough to trust Him with what He allows and trusting Him enough to do things His way. Keeping

your new-found faith in good repair requires a lot of
work, but that is the most important work we have
been assigned.[5]

Putting the Starter Kit to Good Use

Salvation is not just about getting you to heaven as
important as that is. Nor is it primarily about receiving
the forgiveness of your sins as necessary as that is. Nor
is it only about being given a new lease on life, the gift
of the Holy Spirit and a right relationship with Father
God. These are all tremendous gifts to be sure, but they
are only parts of the starter kit.

As one pastor joked, "If all God wanted to do was
save you and get you to heaven, he would have had
one person to lead you to Christ and another right there
to shoot you!" Our Lord has plans to grow us and use
us, both for our delight, the needs of others, and His
glory. To be prepared for all that our new life entails,
put that starter kit you've received to good use while
you are still hanging around the base camp.

There are five very important things, for instance,
that you need to learn how to cultivate by combining
your starter kit with them, because your new life in
Christ depends upon them the way your physical body
depends upon food and water to keep going strong:
Bible, prayer, worship, fellowship and service. We call
these the Big Five Connecters. They are so important
that they require sections of their own.

---

[1] Matthew 6:33: *But seek first the kingdom of God and his righteousness, and all these things will be added to you*; Also Colossians 3:23-24: *Whatever you do, work heartily, as for the Lord and not for men, knowing that from the Lord you will receive the inheritance as your reward. You are serving the Lord Christ.*

[2] We have a major teaching, "The Keys to the Kingdom," at our website for healing, www.healingstreamsusa.org. It's Lesson 3 in the free eCourse for Healing. It is also included in our guide to emotional healing, *The Missing Peace*, available at Amazon.com.

[3] We have a ton of free teachings on the Holy Spirit, including the Baptism of power, at our website for salvation and new life: www.forerunners4him.org. Look under the navigation tab, New Life.

[4] John H. Sammis (1846-1919), lyrics: "Trust and Obey."

[5] John 6:28-29: *Then they said to him, "What must we do, to be doing the works of God?" Jesus answered them, "This is the work of God, that you believe in him whom he has sent."*

THE BIG FIVE CONNECTERS

There are five things that every Christian needs to steadily do in order to stay well-connected to our source: Your life depends upon it! The great thing is that Jesus in you loves doing these five things. They are delights, not duties. If you keep them in good repair, they will keep you powered up and rescue you when you aren't.

Keep These Safety Nets in Play

Jesus is our entry point to both eternal life in heaven and new life on earth. *He is the source of it all!* It is therefore of tremendous, life-saving and life-enhancing importance that we stay connected to the One who is the Way we now live, the Truth we now live by, and the Life we want to experience.

Jesus said to him, "I am the way, and the truth, and the life." John 14:6

Since Jesus says that we can "do nothing" without Him, staying connected is the name of the game.[1] Don't believe me? You have an enemy who never doubts it for a moment. He is relentlessly seeking to get you disconnected![2] To help us in this struggle our God of All Grace has provided five grace-based ways of keeping connected to Himself. He doesn't do them *for* us, but He will do them *with* us—and then work supernaturally through them to keep the connection working.

They are not magical. They do not work automatically. You have to work with them to keep you connected, or they will just become another thing on your list to do, or worse, a source of spiritual pride. They can become rituals or routine if you let them, but beware: All life and delight will seem to go out of them if that's your approach. God won't love you less if you don't do them and He won't love more if you do. You aren't doing these things to please or placate God: *You do them because you want to stay vitally connected to Jesus.*

Why We Need the Big Five

We do the Big Five Connecters for three excellent reasons:

1) Our life in Christ depends upon them. This is how we get connected, stay connected and increase the connection to our source of peace, joy and confidence for living. Just as a battery needs continual recharging to stay powered up, so too we need to stay plugged in to our power source. Our new life streams into us from a source outside of and beyond our own understanding and abilities.

2) They are our meeting place with Jesus. Jesus did all of these five things when He walked the earth. They were His lifeline to the Father and to His true purpose for being on earth. He still loves to do them. That is why they work so well as connecters. He is inside of us now by His Spirit wanting us to gain the

graced-pleasure of doing the Big Five with Him and through Him. These aren't duties—they're delights!

3) They lead us into our destiny. None of us is smart enough to figure out why we're here. That's one of the many reasons why we need a Savior. Jesus told us that we have two primary purposes in life and two assignments that go right along with them. Our primary purpose is to love God whole-heartedly at all times and our secondary purpose is to love others as well as we do ourselves.[3] Our two most important assignments in life are, therefore, to fully accomplish each of those two purposes. The Big Five draw us into our assignments and keep us flowing in those pathways of purpose.[4]

The Danger of Not Doing the Big Five

The important thing to keep in mind is that we are not given these connecters for God's benefit, but for our own. Don't shoot yourself in the foot by ignoring your Big Five lifeline to the Lord. *Think of them as safety nets.* They won't always be in tip-top repair. Sometimes you may neglect one or more of them for fair reasons or foul. When that happens, always be quick to mend them before any sizeable holes develop. You don't want to fall past these "do's" into the "don'ts"!

I have worked with men with addictions for years and have never yet seen someone fall back into the addiction who was faithfully working these five do's. The men, however, almost universally think that the problem was doing the don'ts. Yes, of course we don't want to do the don'ts, but *the do's keep us from the don'ts!*

---

[1] John 15:4-5: *"Abide in me, and I in you. As the branch cannot bear fruit by itself, unless it abides in the vine, neither can you, unless you abide in me. I am the vine; you are the branches. Whoever abides in me and I in him, he it is that bears much fruit, for apart from me you can do nothing."*

[2] 1 Peter 5:8: *Be sober-minded; be watchful. Your adversary the devil prowls around like a roaring lion, seeking someone to devour.*

[3] Matthew 22:37-40: *And he said to him, "You shall love the Lord your God with all your heart and with all your soul and with all your mind. This is the great and first commandment. And a second is like it: You shall love your neighbor as yourself. On these two commandments depend all the Law and the Prophets."*

[4] For more on the Big Five, on our two purposes and all aspects of how to live the new life, see our website www.forerunners4him.org.

CONNECTER 1: THE BIBLE

Think of the Bible as Jesus in written form. He is the Word—God's eternal counsel—made flesh.[1] The Bible is much more than a mere book. It is the living Word of God.[2] Jesus spoke the words that brought all of creation into being. If His spoken Word can do that, think what His written Word can do for you, to bring you fully to life.

Why You Need This Connecter

The Bible isn't an ordinary book. It is composed of 66 separate books written by 40 different authors over a period of 1500 years on three continents in three languages. Yet, it tells a consistent story about God's ways with humanity and our ways with God. That's amazing! Just as amazing is the manuscript trail: Literally thousands of entire copies exist from very ancient times, all with near universal agreement of text. There is nothing else remotely close to this coming to us from antiquity. Truly, the Lord has "watched over His word" to preserve it as well as perform it.[3] Yet, these amazing facts are only the beginning.

According to Peter the whole of scripture is "inspired by God" which means literally God-breathed.[4] The Bible's divine origins set it apart from any other book on the shelf. Jesus used words of scripture to silence the voice of temptation, He taught the Word and lived by the Word throughout His life and ministry; and in His greatest trial just before the cross He declared God's Word to be "truth," praying that we would be "sanctified" by God's word, just as He had been.[5] Being sanctified by the Word means God uses it to cleans us of spiritual darkness and lead us into the light, enabling us to see ourselves and our world from His perspective.

That's a pretty impressive case to make for reading and studying the Bible, but there is even more. Jesus Himself is declared to be the living Word of God, the Word "made flesh."[6] According to His own teaching, the whole of scripture is about Him.[7] In some mysterious way the written Word (scripture) and the living Word (Jesus) are one. In fact the Bible itself is described as living and life-giving, just as Jesus described Himself as both truthful and the Truth.[8]

For the word of God is living and active, sharper than any two-edged sword, piercing to the division of soul and of spirit, of joints and of marrow, and discerning the thoughts and intentions of the heart. Hebrews 4:12 ESV

How It Works as a Safety Net

At the very least the Bible will give you a road map for things to avoid (sins) and for things to do (the Big Five Connecters for instance). Straying outside God's moral boundaries is certain to disconnect you from the One who drew the lines for us in the first place. Trespassing into sin always separates us from God—not from His love—but from our fellowship with Him, from His strong support, and from the confidence and clear conscience He desires to give us. Since that is not what the new you wants to do, you would be wise to get to know the lay of the land from God's perspective in order to stay on the right path. This is the first, most obvious, use of the Bible as a safety net.[9]

The other, more powerful, use of scripture is for staying in communion and communication with God. Jesus is the true source of everything that you need in order to live in peace, joy and God's right ways. The Bible, because it is the written Word, will work to help you stay in close touch with the living Word who is now your Savior and Lord. By His Spirit Jesus will teach you things through the scriptures that you need to know, and then help you believe and do them. He will also use the scriptures to speak to you for comfort, guidance, or correction—we need all three!

As you stay in the scriptures—reading, studying, mediating—the Bible will help keep you connected to Jesus, enjoying a much closer fellowship with Him than you ever could without His Word to bridge the gaps. In this way He will use scripture to help you stay powered up for doing the right thing and also speak through it to wake you up and steer you clear of wrong turns.

Problems to Avoid

The obvious problem to avoid is reading the scriptures too little; less obvious is reading them too much. How can you get too much of a good thing? Spiritual knowledge which the Bible delivers in spades is not the same thing as spiritual growth, which always proves itself out amidst the pressures of daily life. Just as children need both food and exercise in order to grow physically, so we ever-growing Christians need to feed on the word of God and then practice what we are learning, or our growth will be stunted.

The great thing in natural life is to keep up a steady and balanced approach to meals, eating from all the major food groups, while avoiding excessive snacking. Simply opening the Bible to any page or to only your favorite pages is snacking on scripture—not a good strategy for a balanced diet. Find a way of reading the Bible that will take you through whole books and eventually lead you through the whole of scripture. Pick a set time for your meal. Most people choose first thing in the morning. Then have a plan in mind. You could plan to read from cover to cover, for instance, but the "B4 Plan" is my personal favorite (short for four sections of Bible reading). The way this works is that you take four sticky tabs and put one in each of the four basic food groups of scripture:

1) Begin with a bite-size portion of Psalms or Proverbs. Go through these on a loop. Psalms will teach you how to pray and praise, inspire you to love God and help you jump start your heart with devotion each morning. Proverbs will give you practical wisdom for the daily life that lies just ahead. Begin at Psalm 1; when you reach the end of Proverbs 31, circle back around.

2) Then, read a healthy portion of one of the Gospels. These give us our vital images of Jesus. He is God's love in action. He is God's Word to us. He is our Example. Drink Him in. feed on Him. Begin with Matthew; when you get to the end of John, circle back around.

3) Read a portion from the rest of the New Testament. These are letters directed to the churches—that includes us! Naturally, we want to learn from those who knew Jesus best and walked successfully in His ways. Start with any letter you have a hunger to read; read a paragraph or a whole chapter: When you finish that book, move on to another one.

4) Read a portion from the rest of the Old Testament. Clearly it will take more time to eventually finish all of the books that remain, but let your interest—your spiritual hunger—guide you.

Remember to say grace before your spiritual meals: Ask God to open your heart and mind to His Word and to open His Word to your heart and mind. Seek to read from all four groups, but don't beat yourself up if you don't. The important thing is, on the one hand, to keep your spiritual hunger alive by not force feeding yourself according to someone else's schedule and, on the other, to keep chewing your way through a healthy, balanced diet of truth, skipping as few meals as possible. What are you waiting for? Taste and see that the Lord is good![10]

---

[1] John 1:1, 14: *In the beginning was the Word, and the Word was with God, and the Word was God... And the Word became flesh and dwelt among us.*

---

[2] Hebrews 4:12: *For the word of God is living and active, sharper than any two-edged sword, piercing to the division of soul and of spirit, of joints and of marrow, and discerning the thoughts and intentions of the heart.*

[3] Jeremiah 1:12: *Then the Lord said to me, "You have seen well, for I am watching over my word to perform it."*

[4] 2 Peter 1:20-21: *Knowing this first of all, that no prophecy of Scripture comes from someone's own interpretation. For no prophecy was ever produced by the will of man, but men spoke from God as they were carried along by the Holy Spirit.*

[5] John 17:17-19: *Sanctify them in the truth; your word is truth. As you sent me into the world, so I have sent them into the world. And for their sake I consecrate myself, that they also may be sanctified in truth.*

[6] John 1:14: *And the Word became flesh and dwelt among us, and we have seen his glory, glory as of the only Son from the Father, full of grace and truth.*

[7] John 5:39: *You search the Scriptures because you think that in them you have eternal life; and it is they that bear witness about me*; Also Luke 24:44-45: *Then he said to them, "These are my words that I spoke to you while I was still with you, that everything written about me in the Law of Moses and the Prophets and the Psalms must be fulfilled."*

[8] John 6:63: *It is the Spirit Who gives life [He is the Life-giver]; the flesh conveys no benefit whatever [there is no profit in it]. The words (truths) that I have been speaking to you are spirit and life*; John 14:6: *Jesus said to him, "I am the way, and the truth, and the life. No one comes to the Father except through me.*

[9] 2 Timothy 3:16-17 AMP: *Every Scripture is God-breathed (given by His inspiration) and profitable for instruction, for reproof and conviction of sin, for correction of error and discipline in obedience, [and] for training in righteousness (in holy living, in conformity to God's will in thought, purpose, and action), So that the man of God may be complete and proficient, well fitted and thoroughly equipped for every good work.*

[10] Psalm 34:8-10: *Oh, taste and see that the Lord is good! Blessed is the man who takes refuge in him! Oh, fear the Lord, you his saints, for those who fear him have no lack! The young lions suffer want and hunger; but those who seek the Lord lack no good thing.*

CONNECTER 2: PRAYER

We are promised that all who call on His Name will be saved. Prayer is calling on God for mercy, for help or for fellowship. Through prayer the Lord saves us from our sins, our troubles and our aloneness. He delights in listening—no request is too small. Learn to let your need drive you to Him every time: You absolutely cannot wear out the welcome mat. What's more, He has promised to always answer us. Then a true miracle occurs: Prayer takes us through communication into communion.

Why You Need This Connecter

Imagine having someone hanging around you filled with exactly the help, or wisdom, or comfort, or encouragement that you need, but never being allowed to speak to them. That would be incredibly frustrating, wouldn't it? Fortunately it's not that way for us: The Lord positively yearns for us to speak to Him. You don't have to pray: You *get to* pray! Not only is the Lord always willing to listen to your every word, He can actually do something about all of your predicaments. That's reason enough to start talking to Him.

Our need for God's mercy and help extends to every nook and cranny of our lives, as well as that of our loved ones. Interceding—carrying requests to God—is a natural place to begin, once you discover by faith that He is there and that He is listening. Be sure you remember that conversation is a two way street. Learn to wait in silence for Him to speak to you. Even if you don't hear words, you will receive impressions. By these means He communicates understanding, sympathy, and the clear sense that we are not alone. Prayer draws us into intimate fellowship with our best Friend, divine Lover, and majestic Lord. We begin with our short term needs for intercession, but the long term goal is intimacy.

How It Works as a Safety Net

Prayer is our most direct life-line to the Lord. It could take a few moments to phone a friend, your Bible is probably back at the house, a worship service might be days away, but you can always go immediately to God in prayer. In fact He wants you to! He tells us to "come boldly" to His throne anytime we need mercy or His divine assistance.[1] He invites us to call on Him so that He can answer us.[2] And He promises that all who call on His Name will be saved.[3]

When we are under attack by temptations or troubles, we can easily disconnect from God and be carried off the playing field into the land of unhappy outcomes. Don't let that happen: Call on His Name as soon as you sense His peace being lifted off of you. That's the Holy Spirit's way of alerting you to your need to pray. This safety net works for three reasons:

1) As you begin praying hard for God's help, you become occupied with the things of God and that keeps the temptation from gaining ground,

2) God immediately hear" that you really do want His help and starts sending it, and

3) Your preoccupation with prayer eventually shifts your focus off of the tempting thing and back on to a far more desirable thing—your beautiful Lord and Savior. As your focus shifts you become free!

Problems to Avoid

Do not make the mistake of thinking your request or concern is too small—that you shouldn't be troubling the Lord with it. No concern is too small! God really, really loves you, delights in listening to you, and wants to answer your prayers. He may not answer your prayer in the way that you've made it (we don't really know what is best for us), but He will always listen to your heart and treat you right. Don't let false humility hold you back.

Don't become demanding, either. You will eventually discover that your Father will give a good listen to your tears, your fears, even your pain and anger. He seems to welcome the kind of trust that enables us to expose our heart to Him. What doesn't work is becoming strident and stubborn, insisting on our own solution to the problem we are praying about. That's when the heavens can go strangely silent. That's when the Lord seems miles away. Even if you think He has done wrong, He hasn't and He will be gracious and patient in helping you with your feelings. But God will get as quiet as Jesus before Pilate when He is being stubbornly accused. He will simply and silently outwait you. Being eternal, He naturally has time on His side, so don't hold your breath for Him to give in. It's best to walk humbly with your God.

Finally, watch out for falling into routine and ritualized prayers. Would you like someone to talk to you by memorized lines, saying the same thing over and over again? Neither does Jesus! He told us not to pray using vain repetitions.[4] Such prayers are fine for church and may be occasionally helpful in private, but learn to let your conversation be natural, free and wide ranging—just as it would be with a good friend whose affections you cherish and whose wisdom you trust.

---

[1] Hebrews 4:16: *Let us then with confidence draw near to the throne of grace, that we may receive mercy and find grace to help in time of need.*

[2] Jeremiah 33:3: *Call to me and I will answer you, and will tell you great and hidden things that you have not known.*

[3] Romans 10:13: *For "everyone who calls on the name of the Lord will be saved."*

[4] Matthew 6:7 AMP: *And when you pray, do not heap up phrases (multiply words, repeating the same ones over and over) as the Gentiles do, for they think they will be heard for their much speaking.*

CONNECTER 3: WORSHIP

Worship is that higher form of our conversation with the Lord where we are not petitioning Him for what we need, but thanking and praising Him for who He is and what He has already done. This brings us speedily into close communion with Him.[1] We can worship with others in church, in our quiet times, and simply by doing all that we do as a love gift to Him.[2]

Why You Need This Connecter

Worship literally means ascribing worth to the object of our worship.[3] It is so easy for our focus to go off in other directions. Perhaps that is one reason why the Lord structured His Church around a weekly time of worship. In this way He can work with us every seventh day (at least) to get our focus off of ourselves and our problems, and back on to Him. In both public services of worship and private moments of intentionally drawing close to God, we can experience the returning wonder of who He is and of all that He means to us.

Through church services we can learn how to enter His presence with thanksgiving and His courts with praise—and then carry that into our private quiet times as well.[4] Corporate worship creates a spiritual atmosphere which seems to draw heaven closer to the earth, making it easier for everyone present to become worship-full. The Holy Spirit loves to see us worshiping both Father and Jesus and He always comes to carry us higher, once the spirit of true worship moves into our hearts.[5] Don't settle just for singing on key or giving lip service to the prayers. Begin there, but by all means seek to use the collective opening of heaven's portal as an opportunity for you to mount higher into genuine praise and Presence. Put your heart into thanking, praising and adoring God and He will put more of His Heart into you!

We would be missing the mark widely, however, if we only thought of worship as happening in gathered religious meetings or in intimate moments with the Lord. Both of these worship encounters are times set apart from the press and pull of ordinary activity. They can certainly be high points, but there is far more to worship than these special moments. Worship is central to the entirety of our being: We are born worshipers!

In everything that we do we are ascribing worth to something, even if it is the wrong thing. We cannot *not* worship. Sadly, until faith-conversion refocused our hearts, we were worshiping everything else in creation but the One we had been created to worship. The scriptures take the view, however, that everything that we do can be transformed into worship, if it is done for the Lord under His leadership.[6] The telling thing is what is in our heart. If His peace is reigning over us, He has truly been enthroned and rightly worshiped, even in the midst of daily work or play.[7]

How It Works as a Safety Net

Worship services are a gift to us, like shared fire was to those who didn't have it in the old days. At its best a good worship service restores the freshness of experiencing God's presence. When the singing turns into praising, when the praying leads to burdens lifted, when the message becomes a revelation, God is visiting His people. This always refreshes us in the moment and strengthens us for days ahead. *What a lifeline!* And because it is so effective as a safety net, it catches us week after week and holds us in the grip of grace. Strengthened by frequent encounters with our Lord, it is easier to withstand the tempter and stay fired up to pursue our God-given purpose with passion.

A good worship service also serves as a safety net in this way: If we see worship happening around us and cannot enter into it ourselves, then that is a clear sign from the Holy Spirit that we are holding on to something that is holding us back. It may be something we feel guilty about, or worried about; it may be a grudge we are holding against someone. Whatever it is, we need to deal with it and then join in. In this sense I have often compared going to church like going to the doctor. If I'm in good spiritual health, I have no problem entering into the Spirit of worship: That's a clean bill of spiritual health. If not, it's a good thing I had the check-up in time to work on the problem. In fact the presence of the Lord in the worship service not only enables us to see problems (sins), but also conveys grace from Him to overcome them.

Problems to Avoid

We are told that Lucifer once led worship in heaven. He fell due to pride.[8] That should give us all pause. At the very time when he should have been lifting up the Lord and leading others to enthrone God on their praise, Lucifer began lifting up himself, seeking to draw praise attention his way! Jesus also warned us that religious people especially are prone to this problem. The Pharisees loved to be honored, to be seen as holier than others, and to draw praise to themselves. Be very careful about this: Spiritual pride is a terrible pitfall!

Beware also of false humility. Don't hold back because you feel you are unworthy. Jesus has made you worthy to enter God's presence and to stand before Him as a much loved child. We are actually invited to come "boldly" to God's throne of grace anytime we need mercy or help of any kind.[9] Your sinful side will be used by the enemy as an accusation that you are unworthy and unwanted. But these are lies! We run with boldness into His presence, even when we are covered with spiritual slime, because the Blood covers us, the Love invites us, the Spirit unites us, and His Word guarantees a friendly welcome.

---

[1] Psalms 95:2: *Let us come into his presence with thanksgiving; let us make a joyful noise to him with songs of praise!*

[2] Romans 12:1: *I appeal to you therefore, brothers, by the mercies of God, to present your bodies as a living sacrifice, holy and acceptable to God, which is your spiritual worship.*

[3] Our word worship comes from the Old English *weorthscipe* which meant "worthiness, acknowledgment of worth." Oxford Dictionary online.

[4] Psalms 100:4: *Enter his gates with thanksgiving, and his courts with praise! Give thanks to him; bless his name!*

[5] John 4:23 WEB: *But the hour comes, and now is, when the true worshippers will worship the Father in spirit and truth, for the Father seeks such to be his worshippers.*

[6] Romans 12:1-2: *I appeal to you therefore, brothers, by the mercies of God, to present your bodies as a living sacrifice, holy and acceptable to God, which is your spiritual worship. Do not be conformed to this world, but be transformed by the renewal of your mind, that by testing you may discern what is the will of God, what is good and acceptable and perfect.*

[7] Colossians 3:23-24 NASB: *Whatever you do, do your work heartily, as for the Lord rather than for men; knowing that from the Lord you will receive the reward of the inheritance. It is the Lord Christ whom you serve.*

[8] Isaiah 14:12-15 KJV: *How art thou fallen from heaven, O Lucifer, son of the morning! How art thou cut down to the ground, which didst weaken the nations! For thou hast said in thine heart, I will ascend into heaven, I will exalt my throne above the stars of God: I will sit also upon the mount of the congregation, in the sides of the north: I will ascend above the heights of the clouds; I will be like the most High. Yet thou shalt be brought down to hell, to the sides of the pit.*

[9] Hebrews 4:16: *Let us then with confidence draw near to the throne of grace, that we may receive mercy and find grace to help in time of need.*

CONNECTER 4: FELLOWSHIP

Jesus, God the Father and the Holy Spirit are always in perfect love and fellowship with One Another. They are now working through the gospel to draw us out of our self-focus into genuine fellowship with each other and with God.[1] True spiritual fellowship is characterized by close communion with Spirit and truth. By intentionally seeking out friends in the Lord who are also seeking to grow in the right direction, we stay refreshed and strengthened.

Why You Need This Connecter

Fellowship will come as a completely free gift to you at first. You won't have to do anything but open the package! Other believers will welcome you with glad hearts and open arms. They will naturally and easily share their faith with you, pray for your concerns, encourage you and help you find your way. All of this will be exhilarating and immensely comforting: Genuine Christian fellowship is a powerful antidote against loneliness and intimidation. It should open windows of hope as you gain the vision for the Body of Christ on earth being a true family of God's adopted children—the family you have always yearned to know—*a loving, living, breathing expression of Jesus to the world.*

Nothing this good goes unchallenged, so pay attention to "Problems to Avoid." You will definitely have to learn the art of guarding your heart.[2] A well-guarded Christian heart, however, is not like that of a "worldling" or unbeliever.[3] They guard themselves against being hurt by putting up walls and withdrawing from the risk of intimacy with others. It is different for us, once we have learned Jesus' way of forgiving and releasing pain. We guard our hearts by making sure that we are *honest, open and transparent* in our relationships. We embrace living with flawed, imperfect, potentially wounding humanity—just as Jesus did. In this way we learn to seek out fellowship wherever we can find it.

We can enjoy fellowship with all kinds of people and at all kinds of levels of relationship. Why? How? According to scripture we have fellowship with one another "in the truth" and "in the Spirit." [4] Now that we have been born again by Word and Spirit, we are not only free to worship God in Spirit and in truth, we can find common ground with anyone *if* the spirit between us is love *and* we can find some truths to agree upon. This is only hard if you expect perfect love and perfect agreement from everyone you meet. Once you grasp this simple principle you can become well-connected to Jesus practically anytime with practically anyone— especially if they are also seeking fellowship with both you and Jesus.

How It Works as a Safety Net

Intimacy has been described as *in-to-me-see*. The essence of fellowship is being honest, open and transparent in our relationships, especially with the Body of Christ. Through fellowship we *see into* each other and therefore can foresee problems or have

144

insight to things the other person may be facing. In this way fellowship becomes an avenue for wisdom, guidance, correction and confirmation coming to us from the Lord, keeping us on track in our walk with Him. Friends help us get through the difficult patches in life. For this reason scripture compares fellowship to a cord of three strands, one that is not easily broken.[5] Our fellowship with other believers means that if we are honest with them about what we are going through, we can receive the strong support of their prayers, encouragement and practical assistance.

Although our primary reason for going to church is to meet with the Lord in worship, you would be wise to also take advantage of these opportunities for meeting with your *fellows*. Avoid letting your conversations with other believers stay at the level of small talk you could find anywhere. Seek out those who are willing to talk openly about their life in Christ with all of its struggles, hopes and dreams. This is what makes Christian fellowship outstanding; these will be the ones you will want to grow with. Eventually, you may want to cultivate a very close Christian friend, or set of friends, with the intention of meeting regularly, not just by chance. Good friends are among the Lord's best gifts to us; our wise, intentional cultivation of friendships is our gift to them.

Problems to Avoid

Be on your guard! There is a thief who will try to steal the greatest of God's gifts from you.[6] Love is the greatest gift, the one thing that we know we are required to grow. Our hearts should be much bigger by the end of the journey than at the beginning. Fellowship will help you grow love. Even our love for God is put to the test by how we love one another. We learn to love the ones we can see, as evidence that we are also learning to love the One we can't.[7]

Now here's the catch: You cannot grow love without sufficient trust opening and upholding your heart. Your enemy will do his level best to see that you are wounded by your fellow Christians in order to break your trust and cause you to withdraw from close fellowship. Don't let that happen! Being hurt and offended is practically unavoidable. Jesus even said that it was "necessary" that offense come.[8]

Your love has to overcome being offended at the ones who hurt you, mistreat you, fail to measure up and even betray your trust. These will be your greatest opportunities to "grow up into Christ" as you learn to forgive everyone from the heart—just as He does.[9] We need both the pleasurable and the painful side of fellowship to keep growing a heart like Jesus. Never quit and you will be certain to get the hang of loving even the seemingly unlovable.

---

[1] 1 John 1:3: *That which we have seen and heard we proclaim also to you, so that you too may have fellowship with us; and indeed our fellowship is with the Father and with his Son Jesus Christ.*

[2] Proverbs 4:23 AMP: *Keep and guard your heart with all vigilance and above all that you guard, for out of it flow the springs of life.*

[3] The phrase "worldling" indicates someone who is snared by love of the world, rather than love of God: 1 John 2:15 WEB: *Don't love the world,*

neither the things that are in the world. If anyone loves the world, the Father's love isn't in him.

[4] Philippians 2:1 NKJV: *We have fellowship in the Holy Spirit: Therefore if there is any consolation in Christ, if any comfort of love, if any fellowship of the Spirit.* Also 1 John 1:7 NKJV: *We have fellowship in truth (the light): But if we walk in the light as He is in the light, we have fellowship with one another.*

[5] Ecclesiastes 4:9-12: *Two are better than one, because they have a good reward for their toil. For if they fall, one will lift up his fellow. But woe to him who is alone when he falls and has not another to lift him up! Again, if two lie together, they keep warm, but how can one keep warm alone? And though a man might prevail against one who is alone, two will withstand him — a threefold cord is not quickly broken.*

[6] John 10:9: *The thief comes only to steal and kill and destroy. I came that they may have life and have it abundantly.*

[7] 1 John 4:20: *If anyone says, "I love God," and hates his brother, he is a liar; for he who does not love his brother whom he has seen cannot love God whom he has not seen.*

[8] Matthew 18:7 NKJV: *Woe to the world because of offenses! For offenses must come, but woe to that man by whom the offense comes!*

[9] Mark 11:25 WEB: *Whenever you stand praying, forgive, if you have anything against anyone; so that your Father, who is in heaven, may also forgive you your transgressions.*

CONNECTER 5: SERVICE

Serving others leads us out of ourselves into living more like Jesus does—selflessly. Almost everyone has work that they need to do for their own survival which, nevertheless, benefits other people (if it is honest work). Service takes us into the realm where we learn to give ourselves, expecting nothing in return, simply because it is the right and loving thing to do. God always rewards those who follow Jesus in laying down their lives for others.

Why You Need This Connecter

Jesus said that He didn't come to be served, but to serve, even to the point of laying His life down.[1] He saw a world of hurting, needy people, abandoned the easy life in Paradise above and dove into our humanity in order to be of service down here where darkness tramples the earth. He came to seek and save those who were lost. Aren't you glad He found you and now has saved you? So is He! Our Father is a huge Rewarder of anyone who serves His will.[2] He has rewarded Jesus by raising Him to the highest place of joy and honor; He is eager to reward you as well.

Jesus will be working in you by His Spirit to help you become a servant of God. He wants you to get that end-of-life blessing we all covet: "Well done, good and faithful servant."[3] But He also wants you to get the full benefit of becoming like Him *in this life*. He has given you His own servant's heart. A new desire is welling up from your inner depths which (like His) delights in saying to God: "Behold, I have come to do Your will!"[4]

Desiring to be a servant of God's will means that we will be drawn into the good things our loving Father has planned for us, including our destined purpose. Jesus says that as we seek Him first, "all other things" will be added to our life.[5] That's a powerful promise of reward. A further tremendous benefit is that in seeking to be a servant the heart He has given us opens to compassion for others. This draws us out of the terrible bondage of our innate selfishness into experiencing God's kind of selfless love. Being a servant, therefore, transforms us into becoming more like Jesus. This is perhaps the highest reward possible.

How It Works as a Safety Net

Service is very different from ordinary work, but not because it often takes place in a church or through a ministry. It doesn't have to have religious trappings or settings for it to be Christian service. The truth is that anything we do becomes service when it is done *for* the Lord, *through* the Lord and *to* the Lord. Eventually, we can approach even the work we do for money in this way, provided that what we are doing is of actual benefit to others and not immoral or illegal. However, we all have a tendency to self-deceive. Don't imagine that just because you want to do everything for the Lord, you will. Even service for the Lord can become self-serving, if we're not careful.

All legitimate work serves the needs of other people in some way. What separates Christian service from other kinds of work is usually that we are volunteering our time. This provides a powerful check on the way we go at it. In the workplace we can justify having all kinds of attitudes and behaviors while we are slaving for what in the USA is affectionately called the Almighty Dollar. However, when we are seeking to be servants of the Almighty God, our attitudes must match up with those of Jesus. This keeps us honest. If we don't treat people as Jesus would, if we can't keep a good-hearted spirit about us, our service stinks no matter how hard we are working.

Giving your time away in today's material culture only makes sense if you are doing it because you believe the Lord is asking it of you. This is how the call to be of service—in any moment—works as a safety net. If I am not willing to lay my life down or set my agenda aside to be of service to the Lord, or if my attitude proves to be a stinker, then the call to service is showing me I need to have a "come to Jesus" meeting. I may never get that kind of feedback working on my paying job. Service, therefore, works to transform us, if we cooperate.

Problems to Avoid

The main problem to avoid is thinking that God needs your talent. Skills and abilities that you have cultivated, especially in the working world, are indeed God's gifts to you and can be of great benefit in service to Him. But that is not why He called you! It is your heart He wants. If your heart is focused on Him and open with compassion to the needs of others, you are

151

ready to be of good service, no matter what your skills and abilities may be. The Lord needs us teachable and loving, period. He needs our availability far more than our abilities.

To bring us into compliance the Lord may plunge us into something that seems beyond our understanding or capability. This is so that we will learn to rely on Him through prayer and trusting obedience—not ourselves. If you come into a time a service thinking that you already know what needs to be done and how to do it, you will miss the mark by a mile. Don't power up in your own strength or try forcing things under your control. This results in steam-rolling others, losing the peace of Christ, and will bring burn-out in the long run.

The opposite problem, of course, is holding back. Don't let the sight of other people's gifts and abilities make you feel inadequate. You have a heart. You are available. That's all that is really needed! Let God worry about how to put you to good use and how to get the results He wants. It almost always seems like the problem is too big and what we bring to the table is too small. A little boy once showed Andrew two fish and five loaves of bread. Andrew almost didn't bring it to Jesus, yet to everyone's surprise it was all that Jesus needed.[6] That and the faith Andrew had to muster up in order to present so pitiful an offering to the Lord. Step out in faith and the Lord will meet you every time!

[1] Mark 10:43-45: *"But it shall not be so among you. But whoever would be great among you must be your servant, and whoever would be first among you must be slave of all. For even the Son of Man came not to be served but to serve, and to give his life as a ransom for many."*

[2] Colossians 3:23-24: *Whatever you do, work heartily, as for the Lord and not for men, knowing that from the Lord you will receive the inheritance as your reward. You are serving the Lord Christ.*

[3] Matthew 25:23: *"His master said to him, 'Well done, good and faithful servant. You have been faithful over a little; I will set you over much. Enter into the joy of your master.'"*

[4] Hebrews 10:7: *"Then I said, 'Behold, I have come to do your will, O God, as it is written of me in the scroll of the book.'"*

[5] Matthew 6:33: *"But seek first the kingdom of God and his righteousness, and all these things will be added to you."*

[6] John 6:7-10: *Philip answered him, "Two hundred denarii would not buy enough bread for each of them to get a little." One of his disciples, Andrew, Simon Peter's brother, said to him, "There is a boy here who has five barley loaves and two fish, but what are they for so many?" Jesus said, "Have the people sit down."*

HEALING STREAMS MINISTRY

Healing Streams is a ministry of liberation and transformation founded by Steve Evans and his first wife, June, the year before she died. It is now being carried on by Steve and Eunice Evans. Through Biblical teaching we seek to help people find freedom from the negative emotions that rob inner peace and damage health. Our main healing lessons form a 24 part series, *Matters of the Heart*, which can be accessed for free through our website as individual, downloadable teachings in PDF and MP3 formats or viewed on our Youtube channel.

Contact us at
info@healingstreamsusa.org
Visit us on the web at
www.healingstreamsusa.org
www.youtube.com/healingstreamsusa
www.facebook.com/healingstreamsusa

Healing Streams Ministry is a division of Forerunner Ministries, Inc.,
a 501(c)3 nonprofit corporation (Federal Tax ID# 030557651).

THE eCOURSE FOR HEALING
www.healingstreamsusa.org

Practically everyone needs recovery of their heart from some painful issues of the past or could readily benefit from gaining mastery over their emotional turbulence in the present. The peace of Christ is meant to be a river of life that we experience all day long—no matter what our circumstances may be. Let the 24 main healing lessons and workout sessions of our eCourse take your heart on pilgrimage to a place called the Kingdom of God that is already right inside you!

SPIRIT FILLED LIVING IN CHRIST
www.forerunners4Him.org

Whether you are a brand new recruit or a "seasoned veteran", if you find that your peace levels are slipping and your joy is not full, then everything on this site is designed to help you come into the fullness of what it truly means to be saved by grace through faith—in all of your days and all of your situations. And it is all available for free!

For us a forerunner is anyone who receives salvation and begins a lifetime quest of "running" into the heart of God for intimacy and going before the Lord in devoted service to prepare His way into other lives. That's your heart too, isn't it? Come get the equipping you need to be a liberated lover of Jesus and a loving liberator of others.

BOOKS FROM FORERUNNER

If you enjoyed *Salvation Basics*, you can purchase copies for friends at www.createspace.com/4347458 and keep exploring the spiritual life through these other insightful books by Steve Evans, available in paperback and ebook at Amazon.com and Forerunners4Him.org.

Matters of the Heart is a 24 lesson workbook designed
 to guide Christian believers through the basic understandings necessary for releasing emotional damage from the past and gaining a grace-based restoration to wholeness. Each chapter is filled with "tools" for practical application.
278 pages. Paperback: $20.00.

The Missing Peace includes all of the 24 lessons of the
 *Matters of the Heart* teaching series, but without the workbook's other material, focusing instead on a stream of scriptural revelation that will show you how to bring your heart to God and receive His Heart for you in return.
194 pages. Paperback: $15.00.

Rescued from Hell chronicles one man's journey into a
 ten year living nightmare and his astonishing true story of return. Was it an insane delusion or a satanic deception? This is a tale both incredible and terrible, yet studded with life affirming humor and hope-filled insights into the spiritual realities that surround us.
190 pages. Paperback: $12.50.

An Illustrated Guide to the Spiritual Life captures in living color with playful insights the otherwise elusive, invisible realities of our life in God. This "illustrated devotional" includes explanations, scriptures and prayers. It is written for the general reader, but is also a pictorial companion to *The Missing Peace*.

56 pages. Paperback: $10.00.

The River of Peace Series, Vol. 1.

Good Grief is not for everyone, but for those who  despite their pain have "set their hearts on pilgrimage", determined to make it to the other side of the Valley of Tears, allowing sorrow that is *rightly* carried to mend their hearts and guide their lives toward God's new beginning.

70 pages. Paperback: $10.00.

The River of Peace Series, Vol. 2.

Ministry Basics will prepare you to launch into the sea of human need, lostness and misery which surrounds you, finding your place in the Rescue and your highest path of purpose at the Lord's side. Let these field-tested truths equip you for a joy-filled lifetime of Holy Spirit empowered ministry.

163 pages. Paperback: $10.00.

The River of Peace Series, Vol. 4.

28969401R00089

Made in the USA
Middletown, DE
03 February 2016